Cambridge City Election Results since 1935

Introduction

Political parties and their abbreviations

Wards Results

Abbey	1935	2026
Arbury	1968	2026
Castle	1935	2026
Cherry Hinton	1935	2026
Coleridge	1935	2026
East Chesterton	1935	2026
King's Hedges	1976	2026
Market	1935	2026
Newnham	1935	2026
Petersfield	1935	2026
Queen Edith's	1976	2026
Romsey	1935	2026
St Matthew's	1935	1967
Trumpington	1935	2026
West Chesterton	1935	2026

Ward maps

Cambridge City Aldermen 1945-1972

Mayors of Cambridge 1935-2026

Cambridge City Council Leaders since re-organisation in 1973

City of Cambridge Election turnouts

Composition of Cambridge City Council

Index of Cambridge City Councillors

Introduction

The ward election results are given by ward, then date. The candidates are listed in order of votes, with successful candidates in **bold**.

Each ward has (usually) 3 councillors, and these are (usually) elected one at a time, to serve 3 or 4 years.

There have been a few years when the whole council has been elected at once (due to boundary changes, etc.) This is called an "All up election".

If a councillor steps down for any reason, then either there is a byelection, or the next council election will be for 2 places. This means that sometimes elected councillors serve for shorter terms.

This book explains how long a councillor serves, by designating the seats with a number, 1, 2 or 3, given before the name of the elected candidate. So if there is "1" before the name, scan down the list to see the next time that "1" is given, and that will show how long the councillor served.

(R) after a candidate's name means that this is a retiring candidate, standing for re-election. Sometimes this may be someoneretiring from a different ward, or an alderman, which will be specified.

Information in *italics* concerns political parties. *No change* means that the successful candidate is the same party as the retiring candidate (it may, or may not, be the same person). Otherwise it gives which party gained seats. This is important, since it affects the political make-up of the whole council, and may lead to a change of power. The majority of the lowest successful candidate over the highest non-successful candidate is also given, since this shows whether this is a "safe" seat or more marginal.

From time to time, there were re-wardings, where the boundaries of the wards were changed, due to changes in populations of the various wards. Sometimes new wards were created, or an old ward removed. These are indicated in the results. At the end of the results, there are maps showing where the ward boundaries were for each ward.

Political parties and their abbreviations

| Conservatives | *Con* | Conservative |
| | *I.C* | Independent Conservative (all varieties) |

| Labour | *Lab* | Labour |
| | *ILP* | Independent Labour (all varieties) |

"I.C" and "ILP" are used for all unofficial Conservative and Labour candidates.

Liberal and	*NL*	National Liberal (pre-1945)
And Social	*Lib*	Liberal (until 1987)
Democrats	*SDP*	Social Democratic Party (1982-7)
	SLD	Social & Liberal Democrat (1988-9)
	LDm	Liberal Democrat (from 1990)
	Y.L	Young Liberal (1968)

| Greens | *Eco* | Ecology (until 1985) |
| | *Gre* | Green (from 1986) |

Socialists	*SoA*	Socialist Alliance (2002/3)
and	*Rsp*	Respect (2006/7)
Communists	*LfL*	Left List (2008)
	Soc	Cambridge Socialists (2010-3)
	WRP	Workers Revolutionary Party (1982)
	WPB	Workers Party of Britain (2021)
	Comm	Communist
	CPB	Communist Party of Britain (2024)
	YP	Your Party (2025)

Other	*RPA*	Ratepayers' Associations
	USp	United Sports (1992)
	NLP	Natural Law (1995)
	UKIP	UK Independence Party (UKIP)
	WCA	Women Citizens' Association (pre-1945)
	EDm	English Democrats (2008)
	Rnw	Renew (2019)
	Reb	Reboot Democracy (2021)
	Her	Heritage (2023)
	FA	Freedom Alliance (2024)
	Ind	other Independents
	Rfm	Reform UK

~~~ **Abbey** ~~~

November 1935 (All up elections - 3 vacancies)   *3 Con*
1. Henry Arnold (R)	*Con*	841	62.8%	
3. Reuben Elsden (R)	*Con*	796	59.4%	
2. William Stanton (R)	*Con*	768	57.3%	*Con maj 257 (19.2%)*
Alfred Deeks	*Lab*	511	38.1%	
Leonard Doggett	*Lab*	468	34.9%	
Ernest Cutting	*Lab*	456	34.0%	

November 1936   *No change*
2. William Stanton (R)	*Con*	unopposed	

November 1937   *No change*
3. Reuben Elsden (R)	*Con*	550	62.8%	*Con maj 224 (25.6%)*
Leonard Doggett	*Lab*	326	37.2%	

November 1938   *No change*
1. Henry Arnold (R)	*Con*	unopposed	

No elections held during World War II. Arthur Biggs co-opted

November 1945 (2 vacancies)   *2 Lab gains from Con*
2. Ernest Cutting	*Lab*	1018	58.7%	
1. Leonard Wordingham	*Lab*	1006	58.0%	*Lab maj 260 (15.0%)*
Arthur Biggs (R)	*Con*	746	43.0%	
Clifford King	*Con*	698	40.3%	

November 1946   *Lab gain from Con*
3. Alfred Shelley	*Lab*	1073	53.4%	*Lab maj 138 (6.9%)*
Percy North	*Con*	935	46.6%	

November 1947   *Con gain from Lab*
1. Kenneth Gilbert	*Con*	1444	55.8%	*Con maj 302 (11.7%)*
Leonard Wordingham (R)	*Lab*	1142	44.2%	

May 1949   *Con gain from Lab*
2. Harry Habin	*Con*	1291	53.3%	*Con maj 162 (6.7%)*
Ernest Cutting (R)	*Lab*	1129	46.7%	

May 1950   *Con gain from lab*
3. Herbert Finbow	*Con*	1227	50.7%	*Con maj 34 (1.4%)*

Alfred Shelley (R) *Lab* 1193 49.3%

Abbey (contd.)

May 1951   *No change*
1. Kenneth Gilbert (R) *Con* 1446 52.6% *Con maj 145 (5.3%)*
Alfred Shelley   *Lab* 1301 47.4%

May 1952 (2 vacancies)   *2 Lab gains from Con*
2. Ernest Cutting *Lab* 1838 62.5%
1. Phyllis Clark *Lab* 1738 59.1% *Lab maj 551 (18.7%)*
Harry Habin (R) *Con* 1187 40.4%
Sidney West   *Con* 1119 38.0%

May 1953   *Lab gain from Con*
3. P.Jack Warren *Lab* 1628 57.9% *Lab maj 442 (15.7%)*
Herbert Finbow (R) *Con* 1186 42.1%

May 1954   *No change*
1. Phyllis Clark (R) *Lab* 1610 61.5% *Lab maj 603 (23.0%)*
Harry Habin   *Con* 1007 38.5%

May 1955 (2 vacancies)   *No change*
2. Leonard Wordingham *Lab* 1575 56.2% (R) East Chesterton
1. Florence Roden *Lab* 1392 49.7% *Lab maj 52 (1.9%)*
Harry Woolgar   *Con* 1340 47.8%
John Eyles   *Con* 1300 46.4%

May 1956   *No change*
3. P.Jack Warren (R) *Lab* 1465 71.6% *Lab maj 883 (43.1%)*
Arthur Moore   *RPA* 582 28.4%

May 1957   *No change*
1. Dennis Ash *Lab* 1577 66.0% *Lab maj 765 (32.0%)*
Cyril Mercer   *Con* 812 34.0%

May 1958   *No change*
2. Leonard Wordingham (R) *Lab* unopposed

May 1959   *No change*
3. P.Jack Warren (R) *Lab* 1484 63.3% *Lab maj 625 (26.7%)*
Cyril Mercer   *Con* 859 36.7%

May 1960   *No change*
1. Dennis Ash (R) *Lab* unopposed

Abbey (contd.)

July 1960 (byelection)				*No change*
2. John N. Hughes	*Lab*	1039	60.6%	*Lab maj 363 (21.2%)*
Paul Marquis	*Con*	676	39.4%	

May 1961				*No change*
2. John N. Hughes (R)	*Lab*	unopposed		

May 1962				*No change*
3. P.Jack Warren (R)	*Lab*	unopposed		

May 1963				*No change*
1. Dennis Ash (R)	*Lab*	unopposed		

July 1963 (byelection)				*No change*
3. Euphemia Davison	*Lab*	1392	72.3%	*Lab maj 860 (44.7%)*
Phyllis Pink	*Lib*	532	27.7%	

May 1964				*No change*
2. John N. Hughes (R)	*Lab*	unopposed		

July 1964 (byelection)				*No change*
1. Doris Howe	*Lab*	unopposed		

May 1965				*No change*
3. Euphemia Davison (R)	*Lab*	unopposed		

May 1966				*No change*
1. Doris Howe (R)	*Lab*	unopposed		

May 1967				*No change*
2. John N. Hughes (R)	*Lab*	unopposed		

General re-warding: Abbey gained part of St Matthews (which disappeared)

May 1968				*Con gain from Lab*
3. William Goddard	*Con*	968	52.0%	*Con maj 75 (4.0%)*
Euphemia Davison (R)	*Lab*	893	48.0%	

May 1969				*No change*
1. Doris Howe (R)	*Lab*	1020	49.5%	*Lab maj 135 (6.5%)*
Derek Harrison	*Con*	885	42.9%	
David Trotter	*Lib*	157	7.6%	

Abbey (contd.)

May 1970				*No change*
2. John N. Hughes (R)	*Lab*		unopposed	

May 1971				*Lab gain from Con*
3. Alec Molt	*Lab*	1857	73.6%	*Lab maj 1192 (47.3%)*
Sidney Miller	*Con*	665	26.4%	

May 1972				*No change*
1. Doris Howe (R)	*Lab*	1533	92.1%	*Lab maj 1401 (84.1%)*
Shirley Bailey	*Comm*	132	7.9%	

June 1973 (All up elections – 4 vacancies, all retiring 1976)				*4 Lab*
Doris Howe (R)	*Lab*	unopposed		
Alec Molt (R)	*Lab*	unopposed		
O.M.Wendy Nicol (R)	*Lab*	unopposed	(R) Arbury	
P.Jack Warren (R)	*Lab*	unopposed	(R) Alderman	

General re-warding: Abbey lost the area west of the main railway line.

May 1976 (All up elections - 3 vacancies)				*3 Lab*
1. P.Jack Warren (R)	*Lab*	763	53.7%	
3. Doris Howe (R)	*Lab*	671	47.2%	
2. Alec Molt (R)	*Lab*	627	44.1%	*Lab maj 97 (6.8%)*
Edna Jones	*Con*	530	37.3%	
Patricia Allen	*Ind*	168	11.8%	

May 1978				*No change*
2. Alec Molt (R)	*Lab*	830	67.1%	*Lab maj 423 (34.2%)*
Edna Jones	*Con*	407	32.9%	

May 1979				*No change*
3. Doris Howe (R)	*Lab*	2006	59.9%	*Lab maj 1061 (31.7%)*
Edna Jones	*Con*	945	28.2%	
Bernard Greaves	*Lib*	400	11.9%	

May 1980				*No change*
1. Richard Smith	*Lab*	1169	71.6%	*Lab maj 804 (49.2%)*
Edna Jones	*Con*	365	22.4%	
David Green	*Lib*	99	6.1%	

Abbey (contd.)

May 1982				*No change*
2. Carey Widdows	*Lab*	1169	59.2%	*Lab maj 734 (37.1%)*
Else Meyland-Smith	*SDP*	435	22.0%	
Sally-Anne Worland	*Con*	372	18.8%	

May 1983				*No change*
3. Eleanor Fairclough	*Lab*	1167	61.9%	*Lab maj 679 (36.0%)*
Sally-Anne Worland	*Con*	488	25.9%	
Kenneth Hales	*Lib*	230	12.2%	

May 1984				*No change*
1. Richard Smith (R)	*Lab*	1208	62.3%	*Lab maj 658 (33.9%)*
Peter Day	*Con*	550	28.4%	
Don McBey	*SDP*	182	9.4%	

May 1986				*No change*
2. Anthony Barnes	*Lab*	998	59.9%	*Lab maj 592 (35.5%)*
Julie Hayward	*Con*	406	24.4%	
Brian Whitt	*SDP*	263	15.8%	

May 1987				*No change*
3. John Durrant	*Lab*	1069	55.4%	*Lab maj 486 (25.2%)*
Julie Hayward	*Con*	583	30.2%	
Simon Jordan	*Lib*	278	14.4%	

May 1988				*No change*
1. Richard Smith (R)	*Lab*	1096	64.6%	*Lab maj 663 (39.1%)*
Timothy Wheatley	*Con*	433	25.5%	
Barrie Coombes	*SLD*	103	6.1%	
Phillipa Bryan	*Gre*	64	3.8%	

May 1990				*No change*
2. Anthony Barnes (R)	*Lab*	1401	67.0%	*Lab maj 965 (46.1%)*
Sheila Cann	*Con*	436	20.8%	
Stuart Emms	*Gre*	140	6.7%	
Brian Whitt	*LDm*	115	5.5%	

May 1991				No change
3. John Durrant (R)	*Lab*	1050	61.4%	*Lab maj 632 (36.9%)*
Robert Marven	*Con*	418	24.4%	
Brian Whitt	*LDm*	169	9.9%	
Phillipa Bryan	*Gre*	74	4.3%	

Abbey (contd.)

May 1992				*No change*
1. Richard Smith (R)	*Lab*	801	57.6%	*Lab maj 319 (22.9%)*
Joan Hill-Molyneux	*Con*	482	34.7%	
Paul Harden	*LDm*	108	7.8%	

May 1994				*No change*
2. Anthony Barnes (R)	*Lab*	965	66.2%	*Lab maj 712 (48.9%)*
Jeremy Froggett	*Con*	253	17.4%	
Joan Molyneux-Hill	*LDm*	239	16.4%	

May 1995				*No change*
3. John Durrant (R)	*Lab*	988	78.4%	*Lab maj 715 (56.7%)*
Stephanie Langton	*LDm*	273	21.6%	

May 1996				*No change*
1. Richard Smith (R)	*Lab*	882	71.5%	*Lab maj 682 (55.3%)*
Simon Mitton	*Con*	200	16.2%	
Stephanie Langton	*LDm*	151	12.2%	

May 1998				*No change*
2. Mungai Mbayah	*Lab*	578	65.0%	*Lab maj 415 (46.7%) Ind from 2000*
Ann Watkins	*Con*	163	18.3%	
Catherine Stebbings	*LDm*	148	16.6%	

May 1999				*No change*
3. John Durrant (R)	*Lab*	702	71.3%	*Lab maj 545 (55.4%)*
Simon Mitton	*Con*	157	16.0%	
G.Stephen Smith	*LDm*	76	7.7%	
John G Collins	*Gre*	49	5.0%	

May 2000				*No change*
1. Richard Smith (R)	*Lab*	567	62.4%	*Lab maj 343 (37.8%)*
Simon Mitton	*Con*	224	24.7%	
Julian Huppert	*LDm*	117	12.9%	

May 2002				*No change – see Mungai Mbaya 1998*
2. Caroline Hart	*Lab*	571	58.6%	*Lab maj 391 (40.1%)*
Simon Mitton	*Con*	180	18.5%	
Christopher Keating	*LDm*	113	11.6%	
John G Collins	*Gre*	60	6.2%	
Mungai Mbaya (R)	*Ind*	51	5.2%	

Abbey (contd.)

May 2003				*No change*
3. John Durrant (R)	*Lab*	502	55.2%	*Lab maj 307 (33.7%)*
Vivian Ellis	*Con*	195	21.4%	
Thomas Yates	*LDm*	142	15.6%	
John G Collins	*Gre*	71	7.8%	

General re-warding: Abbey regained the Riverside area west of the main railway line.

June 2004 (All up elections - 3 vacancies)				*3 Lab*
2. John Durrant (R)	*Lab*	725	41.8%	
1. Caroline Hart (R)	*Lab*	615	35.5%	
3. Richard Smith (R)	*Lab*	559	32.3%	*Lab maj 171 (9.9%)*
Richard Dutton	*Con*	388	22.4%	
Helen Elsom	*LDm*	360	20.8%	
Edward Sexton	*LDm*	330	19.0%	
Heather Macbeth-Hornett	Gre	322	18.6%	
Simon Mitton	*Con*	322	18.6%	
Magnus Gittins	*Con*	317	18.3%	
Margaret Wright	*Gre*	280	16.2%	
Marcus Streets	*LDm*	279	16.1%	

May 2006				*No change*
3. Miriam Lynn	*Lab*	668	37.4%	*Lab maj 204 (11.4%)*
Margaret Wright	*Gre*	464	26.0%	
Simon Mitton	*Con*	362	20.3%	
Edward Sexton	*LDm*	292	16.3%	

May 2007				*No change*
1. Caroline Hart (R)	*Lab*	701	35.5%	*Lab maj 108 (5.5%)*
Margaret Wright	*Gre*	593	30.0%	
Andrew Bower	*Con*	398	20.1%	
Edward Sexton	*LDm*	284	14.4%	

May 2008				*Gre gain from Lab*
2. Margaret Wright	*Gre*	812	41.4%	*Gre maj 167 (8.5%)*
John Durrant (R)	*Lab*	645	32.9%	
Andrew Bower	*Con*	376	19.2%	
Callie Leroux	*LDm*	129	6.6%	

Abbey (contd.)

May 2010				*Gre gain from Lab*
3. Adam Pogonowski	*Gre*	1104	29.7%	*Gre maj 94 (2.5%) Lab from 2012*
Christopher Brown	*LDm*	1010	27.2%	
George Owers	*Lab*	848	22.8%	
Lara Hillman	*Con*	758	20.4%	

May 2011				*No change*
1. Caroline Hart (R)	*Lab*	1057	41.8%	*Lab maj 261 (10.3%)*
Brett Hughes	*Gre*	796	31.5%	
Craig Thomas	*Con*	414	16.4%	
Christopher Brown	*LDm*	260	10.3%	

May 2012				*Lab gain from Gre*
2. Richard Johnson	*Lab*	963	54.4%	*Lab maj 540 (30.5%)*
William Birkin	*Gre*	423	23.9%	
Timothy Haire	*Con*	219	12.4%	
Christopher Brown	*LDm*	165	9.3%	

May 2013 (byelection)				*No change*
3. Peter Roberts	*Lab*	878	51.4%	*Lab maj 542 (31.8%)*
Oliver Perkins	*Gre*	336	19.7%	
Eric Barrett-Payton	*Con*	284	16.6%	
Marcus Streets	*LDm*	209	12.2%	

May 2014				*No change*
3. Peter Roberts (R)	*Lab*	1130	48.7%	*Lab maj 650 (28.0%)*
Oscar Gillespie	*Gre*	480	20.7%	
Marcus Streets	*LDm*	384	16.5%	
Eric Barrett-Payton	*Con*	328	14.1%	

May 2015				*No change*
1. Caroline Hart (R)	*Lab*	1645	42.5%	*Lab maj 814 (21.0%)*
Nichola Martin	*LDm*	831	21.5%	
Monica Hone	*Gre*	701	18.1%	
David Cowan	*Con*	696	18.0%	

May 2016				*No change*
2. Richard Johnson (R)	*Lab*	1235	61.3%	*Lab maj 943 (46.8%)*
Monica Hone	*Gre*	292	14.5%	
Nicky Shepard	*LDm*	266	13.2%	
Angela Ozturk	*Con*	222	11.0%	

May 2018   *No change*
3. Nicky Massey   *Lab*   1283   57.0%   *Lab maj 817 (36.3%)*
Nicky Shepard   *LDm*   466   20.7%
David Smith   *Con*   263   11.7%
Naomi Bennett   *Gre*   240   10.7%

May 2019   *No change*
1. Haf Davies   *Lab*   1055   50.0%   *Lab maj 578 (27.4%)*
Naomi Bennett   *Gre*   477   22.6%
Jake Butt   *LDm*   328   15.6%
David Smith   *Con*   179   8.5%
Boris Boyd   *Rnw*   69   3.3%

No elections in 2020 due to Covid-19 pandemic

General re-warding (see map, near end of book)

May 2021 (All up elections – 3 vacancies)   *2 Gre 1 Lab*
1. Naomi Bennett   *Gre*   1178   41.3%
2. Hannah Copley   *Gre*   1144   40.2%
3. Haf Davies (R)   *Lab*   1090   38.3%   *Lab maj 57 (2.0%)*
Matt Howard   *Gre*   1033   36.3%
Richard Johnson (R)   *Lab*   1029   36.1%
Nicky Massey (R)   *Lab*   1014   35.6%
Timothy Haire   *Con*   299   10.5%
Elizabeth Parkin   *LDm*   270   9.5%
Geoffrey Owen   *Con*   236   8.3%
Paul Roper   *Con*   234   8.2%
Sophie West   *LDm*   199   7.0%
Zoe Zhang   *LDm*   149   5.2%

May 2022   *Gre gain*
3. Matthew Howard   *Gre*   1254   48.0%   *Gre maj 280 (10.7%)*
Amanda Hawkes   *Lab*   974   37.3%
David Smith   *Con*   201   7.7%
Rosemary Ansell   *LDm*   184   7.0%

May 2023   *No change*
2. Elliot Tong   *Gre*   1077   42.8%   *Gre maj 273 (10.8%)*
Zarina Anwar   *Lab*   804   31.9%
David Smith   *Con*   463   18.4%
Rosemary Ansell   *LDm*   174   6.9%

Abbey (contd.)

May 2024				*No change*
1.Naomi Bennett (R}	*Gre*	1189	52.1%	*Gre maj 539 (23.6%)*
Ben Cartwright	*Lab*	650	28.5%	
David Smith	*Con*	226	9.9%	
Rosie Ansell	*LDm*	173	7.6%	
Simon Brignell	*CPB*	42	1.8%	

May 2026				*No change*
Maria Cleminson	*Gre*	1374	51.4%	*Gre maj 919 (34.4%)*
Ruaidhri O'Donnell	*Lab*	455	17.0%	
Tommy Brace	*Rfm*	365	13.6%	
Rosemary Ansell	*LDm*	302	11.3%	
David Smith	*Con*	161	6.0%	
Simon Brignell	*CPB*	17	0.6%	

~~~ **Arbury** ~~~

Ward created in 1968.
Initially represented by councillors elected for St Matthew's, recently abolished:
Rev.Victor Dixon (*Ind*), Clarissa Kaldor (*Lab*), Anthony Cornell (*Con*)

May 1968				*Con gain from Ind*
2. Brian George	*Con*	1538	62.3%	*Con maj 609 (24.7%)*
Gwyneth Lipstein	*Lab*	929	37.7%	

May 1969				*Con gain from Lab*
3. Sidney Reid	*Con*	1161	40.2%	*Con maj 214 (7.4%)*
Clarissa Kaldor (R)	*Lab*	947	32.8%	
Bernard Cornell	*Ind*	648	22.4%	
Anne Miller	*Lib*	133	4.6%	

May 1970				*Lab gain from Con*
1. Clarissa Kaldor	*Lab*	1876	55.9%	*Lab maj 394 (11.7%)*
Anthony Cornell (R)	*Con*	1482	44.1%	

May 1971				*Lab gain from Con*
2. Robert Woods	*Lab*	2324	65.3%	*Lab maj 1091 (30.7%)*
Brian George (R)	*Con*	1233	34.7%	

May 1972				*Lab gain from Con*
3. O.M.Wendy Nicol	*Lab*	2285	66.8%	*Lab maj 1149 (33.6%)*
Sidney Reid (R)	*Con*	1136	33.2%	

June 1973 (All up elections - 4 vacancies, all retiring 1976)				4 *Lab*
Clarissa Kaldor (R)	*Lab*	1662	82.6%	
Robert Woods (R)	*Lab*	1613	80.1%	
Peter Cowell	*Lab*	1606	79.8%	
Elizabeth Peel	*Lab*	1539	76.4%	*Lab maj 937 (46.5%)*
Jacqueline George	*Con*	602	29.9%	
Sidney Miller	*Con*	540	26.8%	
Terence Skipp	*Con*	491	24.4%	

General re-warding: The northern part of Arbury formed the new ward of King's Hedges. Part of Castle Ward between Histon Rd and Stretten Ave was added.

Arbury (contd.)

May 1976 (All up elections - 3 vacancies)				*3 Lab*
1. Elizabeth Gard	*Lab*	1160	46.8%	(R) Newnham
3. Michael Rooney	*Lab*	1127	45.5%	(R) East Chesterton
2. L.Ann Pettifor	*Lab*	1118	45.2%	*Lab maj 25 (1.0%)*
Olive Green	*Con*	1093	44.1%	
Stanley Tyrrell	*Con*	1089	44.0%	
John Newman	*Con*	1084	43.8%	

May 1978				*No change*
2. Barbara May	*Lab*	1314	53.7%	*Lab maj 179 (7.3%)*
Sheila Jones	*Con*	1135	46.3%	

May 1979				*No change*
3. Edward Cowell	*Lab*	1797	44.9%	*Lab maj 231 (5.8%)*
Patrick Harris	*Con*	1566	39.2%	
Robert Arbon	*Lib*	636	15.9%	

May 1980				*No change*
1. Elizabeth Gard (R)	*Lab*	1272	52.6%	*Lab maj 350 (14.5%)*
Patrick Harris	*Con*	922	38.2%	
Charles Burch	*Lib*	222	9.2%	

May 1982				*No change*
2. Stephen Watts	*Lab*	1058	39.2%	*Lab maj 204 (7.6%)*
Stephen George	*Con*	854	31.7%	
Philip Laidlaw	*SDP*	785	29.1%	

May 1983				*No change*
3. Edward Cowell (R)	*Lab*	1305	47.1%	*Lab maj 412 (14.9%)*
Stephen George	*Con*	893	32.2%	
Philip Laidlaw	*SDP*	572	20.6%	

May 1984				*No change*
1. Elizabeth Gard (R)	*Lab*	1093	46.8%	*Lab maj 352 (15.1%)*
Susan Pilkington	*Con*	741	31.7%	
Peter Warner	*SDP*	501	21.5%	

May 1986				*No change*
2. Marie Thompson	*Lab*	1041	47.3%	*Lab maj 369 (16.8%)*
M.Sylvia Davenport	*Con*	672	30.5%	
Karen Burgess	*Lib*	487	22.1%	

Arbury (contd.)

May 1987				*No change*
3. Peter Chaplin	*Lab*	959	39.7%	*Lab maj 68 (2.8%)*
M.Sylvia Davenport	*Con*	891	36.9%	
Alison Pegrum	*SDP*	563	23.3%	

May 1988				*No change*
1. Elizabeth Gard (R)	*Lab*	1100	51.8%	*Lab maj 307 (14.4%)*
Sylvia Davenport	*Con*	793	37.3%	
Evelyn Corder	*SLD*	232	10.9%	

May 1990				*No change*
2. Marie Thompson (R)	*Lab*	1343	54.4%	*Lab maj 656 (26.6%)*
Julia Clark	*Con*	687	27.8%	
Evelyn Corder	*LDm*	294	11.9%	
Simon Ounsworth	*Gre*	145	5.9%	

May 1991				*No change*
3. Sandra Wilson	*Lab*	1034	48.0%	*Lab maj 379 (17.6%)*
Vivian Ellis	*Con*	655	30.4%	
Evelyn Corder	*LDm*	466	21.6%	

May 1992				*Con gain from Lab*
1. Vivian Ellis	*Con*	931	45.4%	*Con maj 76 (3.7%)*
Elizabeth Gard (R)	*Lab*	855	41.7%	
Alison Pegrum	*LDm*	265	12.9%	

May 1994				*No change*
2. Anthony Colombo	*Lab*	1200	53.3%	*Lab maj 617 (27.4%)*
Thomas McGuire	*Con*	583	25.9%	
Adrian Wrigley	*LDm*	467	20.8%	

May 1995				*No change*
3. Robin Horne	*Lab*	1180	61.2%	*Lab maj 742 (38.5%)*
Stephen George	*Con*	438	22.7%	
Adrian Wrigley	*LDm*	310	16.1%	

May 1996				*Lab gain from Con*
1. H.Patricia Wright	*Lab*	1063	54.9%	*Lab maj 393 (20.3%)*
Vivian Ellis (R)	*Con*	670	34.6%	
Adrian Wrigley	*LDm*	205	10.6%	

Arbury (contd.)

May 1997 (byelection)				*No change*
2. Anthony Schofield	*Lab*	1769	51.3%	*Lab maj 663 (19.2%)*
Mark J. Taylor	*Con*	1106	32.1%	
Tim Wesson	*LDm*	571	16.6%	

May 1998				*No change*
2. Anthony Schofield (R)	*Lab*	676	53.2%	*Lab maj 281 (22.1%)*
Mark J. Taylor	*Con*	395	31.1%	
Rhodri James	*LDm*	199	15.7%	

May 1999				*No change*
3. Robin Horne (R)	*Lab*	775	57.2%	*Lab maj 394 (29.1%)*
Mark J. Taylor	*Con*	381	28.1%	
Rhodri James	*LDm*	198	14.6%	

February 2000 (byelection)				*LDm gain from Lab*
3. Rhodri James	*LDm*	723	44.5%	*LDm maj 183 (11.3%)*
Stuart Newbold	*Lab*	540	33.2%	
Mark J. Taylor	*Con*	312	19.2%	
Stephen Lawrence	*Gre*	51	3.1%	

May 2000				*LDm gain from Lab*
1. Timothy Ward	*LDm*	691	35.5%	*LDm maj 36 (1.8%)*
H.Patricia Wright (R)	*Lab*	655	33.6%	
Robert Boorman	*Con*	544	27.9%	
Stephen Lawrence	*Gre*	57	2.9%	

May 2002				*No change*
2. Michael Todd-Jones	*Lab*	828	41.0%	*Lab maj 249 (12.3%)*
Rupert Moss-Eccardt	*LDm*	579	28.7%	
Robert Boorman	*Con*	513	25.4%	
Shayne Mitchell	*Gre*	73	3.6%	
Diana Minns	*SoA*	27	1.3%	

May 2003				*No change*
3. Rhodri James (R)	*LDm*	739	36.4%	*LDm maj 50 (2.5%)*
Ian Kidman	*Lab*	689	33.9%	
Robert Boorman	*Con*	535	26.3%	
Peter Pope	*Gre*	70	3.4%	

General re-warding: Arbury gained the eastern part of Castle and lost Arbury Court to King's Hedges and Bateson Road to West Chesterton.

June 2004 (All up elections - 3 vacancies)   *3 LDm*

2. Rhodri James (R)	*LDm*	1167	39.9%	
1. Anthony Hymans	*LDm*	1004	34.3%	
3. Timothy Ward (R)	*LDm*	976	33.4%	*LDm maj 68 (2.3%)*
Michael Todd-Jones (R)	*Lab*	908	31.1%	
Ian Kidman	*Lab*	900	30.8%	
Janet Robertson-Forrest	*Lab*	777	26.6%	
Robert Boorman	*Con*	699	23.9%	
Rhona Boorman	*Con*	662	22.6%	
Shapour Meftah	*Con*	544	18.6%	
Edwina Wood	*Gre*	459	15.7%	

May 2006   *No change*

3. Timothy Ward (R)	*LDm*	1022	40.3%	*LDm maj 500 (11.9%)*
Michael Todd-Jones	*Lab*	816	32.1%	
Shapour Meftah	*Con*	482	19.0%	
Michael Smith	*Gre*	219	8.6%	

May 2007   *No change*

1. Alan Levy	*LDm*	887	35.8%	*LDm maj 12 (0.5%)*
Michael Todd-Jones	*Lab*	875	35.3%	
Shapour Meftah	*Con*	504	20.3%	
Michael Smith	*Gre*	211	8.5%	

May 2008   *Lab gain from LDm*

2. Michael Todd-Jones	*Lab*	941	35.3%	*Lab maj 33 (1.2%)*
Rhodri James (R)	*LDm*	908	34.1%	
Shapour Meftah	*Con*	468	17.6%	
Catherine Terry	*Gre*	187	7.0%	
Tim Hawke	*EDm*	161	6.0%	

May 2010   *No change*

3. Timothy Ward (R)	*LDm*	1633	38.9%	*LDm maj 500 (11.9%)*
Ian Kidman	*Lab*	1133	27.0%	
Ali Meftah	*Con*	812	19.3%	
Stephen Lawrence	*Gre*	620	14.8%	

Arbury (contd.)

May 2011				*Lab gain*
1. Carina O'Reilly	*Lab*	1310	40.5%	*Lab maj 295 (9.1%)*
Alan Levy (R)	*LDm*	1015	31.4%	
Ali Meftah	*Con*	448	13.8%	
Stephen Lawrence	*Gre*	377	11.6%	
Albert Watts	*UKIP*	87	2.7%	

May 2012				*No change*
2. Michael Todd-Jones (R)	*Lab*	1322	59.9%	*Lab maj 905 (41.0%)*
Rhodri James	*LDm*	417	18.9%	
Ali Meftah	*Con*	237	10.7%	
Stephen Lawrence	*Gre*	232	10.5%	

May 2014				*Lab gain from LDm*
3. Charlotte Perry	*Lab*	1300	45.6%	*Lab maj 578 (20.3%)*
Tim Ward (R)	*LDm*	722	25.3%	
Stephen Lawrence	*Gre*	444	15.6%	
T.James Mottram	*Con*	385	13.5%	

May 2015				*No change*
1. Carina O'Reilly (R)	*Lab*	1673	39.1%	*Lab maj 508 (11.9%)*
Tim Ward	*LDm*	1165	27.2%	
Eric Barrett-Payton	*Con*	597	13.9%	
Stephen Lawrence	*Gre*	568	13.3%	
Celia Conway	*UKIP*	281	6.6%	

May 2016				*No change*
2. Michael Todd-Jones (R)	*Lab*	1430	61.5%	*Lab maj 1062 (45.7%)*
Tim Ward	*LDm*	368	15.8%	
James Strachan	*Con*	282	12.1%	
Stephen Lawrence	*Gre*	245	10.5%	

May 2017 (byelection)				*No change*
3. Patrick Sheil	*Lab*	1267	46.8%	*Lab maj 275 (10.2%)*
Tim Ward	*LDm*	992	36.6%	
Henry Collins	*Con*	450	16.6%	

May 2018				*No change*
3. Patrick Sheil (R)	*Lab*	1250	51.8%	*Lab maj 655 (27.1%)*
Tim Ward	*LDm*	595	24.6%	
Dylan Coll-Reed	*Con*	351	14.5%	
Stephen Lawrence	*Gre*	219	9.1%	

Arbury (contd.)

May 2019   *No change*
1. Carina O'Reilly (R)	*Lab*	1097	48.9%	*Lab maj 543 (24.2%)*
Tim Ward	*LDm*	554	24.7%	
Stephen Lawrence	*Gre*	351	15.7%	
Hary Clynch	*Con*	240	10.7%	

No elections in 2020 due to Covid-19 pandemic

General re-warding (see map, near end of book)

May 2021 (All up elections – 3 vacancies)   *3 Lab*
1. Carina O'Reilly (R)	*Lab*	1241	48.9%	
2. Mike Todd-Jones (R)	*Lab*	1106	43.6%	
3. Patrick Sheil (R)	*Lab*	1006	39.6%	*Lab maj 457 (18.0%)*
Tim Ward	*LDm*	549	21.6%	
Tracy Bend	*Gre*	469	18.5%	
Katrina Barnes	*Gre*	464	18.3%	
Hannah Whitehouse	*LDm*	439	17.3%	
Rory Clark	*LDm*	387	15.2%	
Stephen Lawrence	*Gre*	342	13.5%	
Robert Boorman	*Con*	339	13.4%	
Rhona Boorman	*Con*	324	12.8%	
Ian Gregory	*Con*	293	11.5%	
Keith Garrett	*Reb*	63	2.5%	

May 2022 - 2 vacancies   *No change*
3. Iva Divkovic	*Lab*	1176	52.2%	
1. Patrick Sheil (R)	*Lab*	1145	50.8%	*Lab maj 701 (31.1%)*
Fionna Tod	*LDm*	444	19.7%	
Tim Ward	*LDm*	423	18.8%	
Stephen Lawrence	*Gre*	366	16.2%	
Robert Boorman	*Con*	317	14.1%	
Peter Pope	*Gre*	292	12.9%	
Timothy Haire	*Con*	242	10.7%	

May 2023   *No change*
2. Mike Todd-Jones(R)	*Lab*	1175	48.1%	*Lab maj 504 (20.6%)*
Robert Boorman	*Con*	671	27.5%	
Stephen Lawrence	*Gre*	333	13.6%	
Sam Oliver	*LDm*	264	10.8%	

Arbury (contd.)

May 2024					*No change*
1.Patrick Sheil (R)	*Lab*	1093	51.5%	*Lab maj 728 (34.3%)*
Robert Boorman	*Con*	365	17.2%	
Stephen Lawrence	*Gre*	348	16.4%	
John Leighton	*LDm*	316	14.9%	

May 2026					*Gre gain*
Sefira Davison	*Gre*	928	32.2%	*Gre maj 112 (3.9%)*
Jocelynne Scutt	*Lab*	816	28.3%	
Fionna Tod	*LDm*	667	23.1%	
Will Burrows	*Rfm*	290	10.0%	
Robert Boorman	*Con*	185	6.4%	

~~~ **Castle** ~~~

November 1935 (All up elections - 3 vacancies)   *Ind, Con, NL*

1. William Wing (R)	*Ind*	1007	57.9%	
3. Francis Doggett	*Con*	820	47.2%	*(R) W.Chesterton*
2. William Swift	*NL*	742	42.7%	*NL maj 98 (5.6%) (R) W.Chesterton*
Gordon Frost	*Con*	644	37.0%	
Dorothy Needham	*Lab*	517	29.7%	
Arthur Case	*Lab*	443	25.5%	

November 1936   *No change*

2. William Swift (R)	*NL*	1007	69.4%	*NL maj 564 (38.9%)*
Dorothy Needham	*Lab*	443	30.6%	

November 1937   *No change*

3. Francis Doggett (R)	*Con*	unopposed	

November 1938   *No change*

1. William Wing (R)	*Ind*	unopposed	

No elections held during World War II.

November 1945   *Ind gain from Con*

2. Howard Mallett	*Ind*	1111	50.1%	*Ind maj 4 (0.2%)*
Arthur Cross	*Lab*	1107	49.9%	

November 1946   *No change*

3. Francis Doggett (R)	*Con*	1935	64.9%	*Con maj 889 (29.8%)*
Robert Fordham	*Lab*	1046	35.1%	

November 1947   *Con gain from Ind*

1. Cecil Mole	*Con*	1897	59.0%	*Con maj 1158 (36.0%)*
Louis Dexter	*Lab*	739	23.0%	
Jane Salter	*Ind*	579	18.0%	

December 1947 (byelection)   *No change*

3. Bertram White	*Con*	1411	69.7%	*Con maj 799 (39.5%)*
Louis Dexter	*Lab*	612	30.3%	

May 1949   *No change (see 1945)*

2. Howard Mallett (R)	*Con*	1999	68.8%	*Con maj 1093 (37.6%)*
Robert Fordham	*Lab*	906	31.2%	

Castle (contd.)

May 1950				*No change*
3. Bertram White (R)	*Con*	1516	70.1%	*Con maj 868 (40.1%)*
George Clark	*Lib*	648	29.9%	

May 1951				*No change*
1. Cecil Mole (R)	*Con*	unopposed		

May 1952				*No change*
2. Howard Mallett (R)	*Con*	1750	59.9%	*Con maj 579 (19.8%)*
Arthur Cobb	*Lab*	1171	40.1%	

May 1953				*No change*
3. Bertram White (R)	*Con*	1521	65.4%	*Con maj 717 (30.8%)*
Raymond Flack	*Lab*	804	34.6%	

May 1954				*No change*
1. Cecil Mole (R)	*Con*	unopposed		

May 1955				*No change*
2. Howard Mallett (R)	*Con*	unopposed		

May 1956				*No change*
3. Bertram White (R)	*Con*	1095	69.9%	*Con maj 624 (39.8%)*
Donald Millard	*Lab*	471	30.1%	

May 1957 (2 vacancies)				*No change*
1. Cecil Mole (R)	*Con*	1423	68.2%	
2. George Dean	*Con*	1376	65.9%	*Con maj 662 (31.7%)*
Florence Roden	*Lab*	714	34.2%	(R) Abbey
Donald Millard	*Lab*	663	31.8%	

May 1958				*No change*
2. George Dean (R)	*Con*	983	41.5%	*Con maj 112 (4.7%)*
Horace Ives	*Lib*	871	36.7%	
Gladys Flack	*Lab*	517	21.8%	

May 1959				*Lib gain from Con*
3. Horace Ives	*Lib*	1023	47.8%	*Lib maj 53 (2.5%)*
Bertram White (R)	*Con*	970	45.4%	
John Clark	*ILP*	145	6.8%	

Castle (contd.)

May 1960				*No change*
1. Cecil Mole (R)	*Con*	1257	84.9%	*Con maj 1033 (69.8%)*
Reuben Holland	*Ind*	224	15.1%	

May 1961				*No change*
2. George Dean (R)	*Con*	1112	84.9%	*Con maj 914 (69.8%)*
Reuben Holland	*Ind*	198	15.1%	

May 1962				*No change*
3. Horace Ives (R)	*Lib*	1108	51.9%	*Lib maj 375 (17.6%)*
Dorothy Lockyer	*Con*	733	34.4%	
Reuben Holland	*Lab*	292	13.7%	

May 1963				*Lib gain from Con*
1. Claude Rivers	*Lib*	939	43.2%	*Lib maj 110 (5.1%)*
Isabell Howell	*Con*	829	38.1%	
Raymond Flack	*Lab*	407	18.7%	

May 1964				*No change*
2. George Dean (R)	*Con*	943	39.1%	*Con maj (83 3.4%)*
M.Joan Fitch	*Lib*	860	35.7%	
Frank Symons	*Lab*	606	25.2%	

June 1964 (byelection)				*Con gain from Lib*
3. Stuart Hemsley	*Con*	732	51.0%	*Con maj 30 (2.1%)*
M.Joan Fitch	*Lib*	702	49.0%	

May 1965				*No change*
3. Stuart Hemsley (R)	*Con*	1230	58.4%	*Con maj 353 (16.8%)*
M.Joan Fitch	*Lib*	877	41.6%	

May 1966				*Con gain from Lib*
1. Edward Harmer	*Con*	1036	43.4%	*Con maj 315 (13.2%)*
Peter Knowlson	*Lib*	721	30.2%	
Rosemary Crompton	*Lab*	628	26.3%	

November 1966 (byelection)				*No change*
3. Neville Auker	*Con*	891	55.8%	*Con maj 185 (11.6%)*
Peter Knowlson	*Lib*	706	44.2%	

May 1967				*No change*
2. George Dean (R)	*Con*	unopposed		

Castle (contd.)

July 1967 (byelection)   *No change*
2. John Powley   *Con*   unopposed

General rewarding: Castle lost area to Newnham, West Chesterton and the new Arbury.

May 1968   *No change*
3. Neville Auker (R)   *Con*   1507   67.0%   *Con maj 764 (34.0%)*
Dorothy Silberston   *Lab*   743   33.0%

May 1969   *No change*
1. Edward Harmer (R)   *Con*   1464   67.5%   *Con maj 760 (35.1%)*
Dorothy Silberston   *Lab*   704   32.5%

May 1970   *No change*
2. John Powley (R)   *Con*   1259   75.0%   *Con maj 839 (50.0%)*
Josie Ding   *Lab*   420   25.0%

May 1971   *No change*
3. Neville Auker (R)   *Con*   1312   54.5%   *Con maj 215 (8.9%)*
O.M.Wendy Nicol   *Lab*   1097   45.5%

May 1972   *No change*
1. Edward Harmer (R)   *Con*   1210   50.6%   *Con maj 28 (1.2%)*
Stephen Watson   *Lab*   1182   49.4%

June 1973 (All up elections – 3 vacancies, all retiring 1976)   *3 Con*
Neville Auker (R)   *Con*   1121   55.9%
Brian George   *Con*   1063   53.0%
John Powley (R)   *Con*   1061   52.9%   *Con maj 122 (6.1%)*
Robert Prescott   *Lab*   939   46.8%
Stephen Lack   *Lab*   925   46.1%
Noeline Sargent   *Lab*   906   45.2%

General re-warding: Castle lost the area east of Histon Road to Arbury; gained that south of Victoria Road, and that southwest of Huntingdon Road.

Castle (contd.)

May 1976 (All up elections – 3 vacancies)				*3 Con*
1. Neville Auker (R)	*Con*	1550	57.8%	
3. John Powley (R)	*Con*	1487	55.5%	
2. George Reid	*Con*	1449	54.1%	*Con maj 449 (16.8%)*
Myles Mackie	*Lab*	1000	37.3%	
Margaret Wilson	*Lab*	987	36.8%	
Josef Schicker	*Lab*	976	36.4%	

May 1978				*No change*
2. George Reid (R)	*Con*	1082	44.0%	*Con maj 240 (9.8%)*
Richard Kimber	*Lab*	842	34.2%	
Andrew Gore	*Lib*	537	21.8%	

May 1979				*Lib gain from Con*
3. David Pickles	*Lib*	2148	49.9%	*Lib maj 995 (23.1%)*
John Powley (R)	*Con*	1153	26.8%	
Edwin Mortlock	*Lab*	1003	23.3%	

May 1980				*Lib gain from Con*
1. Alan Charlesworth	*Lib*	1162	43.5%	*Lib maj 178 (6.7%)*
Neville Auker (R)	*Con*	984	36.9%	
Joan Robinson	*Lab*	524	19.6%	

May 1982				*Lib gain from Con*
2. Andrew Duff	*Lib*	1300	46.3%	*Lib maj 233 (8.3%)*
George Reid (R)	*Con*	1067	38.0%	
Richard Newbury	*Lab*	440	15.7%	

May 1983				*No change*
3. David Pickles (R)	*Lib*	1425	45.9%	*Lib maj 348 (11.2%)*
George Reid	*Con*	1077	34.7%	
Vivien Allum	*Lab*	605	19.5%	

May 1984				*No change*
1. Alan Charlesworth (R)*Lib*		1261	44.3%	*Lib maj 313 (11.0%)*
Kate French	*Con*	948	33.3%	
Mark Adams	*Lab*	637	22.4%	

May 1986				*No change*
3. Andrew Duff (R)	*Lib*	1221	42.1%	*Lib maj 276 (9.5%)*
Peter Hoskins	*Con*	945	32.6%	
Jonathan Megginson	*Lab*	734	25.3%	

Castle (contd.)

May 1987				*No change*
3. David Howarth	*Lib*	1470	43.8%	*Lib maj 317 (9.4%)*
Robert Gregory	*Con*	1153	34.4%	
Jessie Ball	*Lab*	733	21.8%	

May 1988				*Con gain from Lib*
1. Robert Gregory	*Con*	1058	34.9%	*Con maj (10 0.3%)*
Jane Bays	*SLD*	1048	34.5%	
Jessie Ball	*Lab*	928	30.6%	

May 1990				*No change*
2. Alan Charlesworth	*LDm*	1139	33.6%	*LDm maj 125 (3.7%)*
Kevin Price	*Lab*	1014	29.9%	
June Saunders	*Con*	983	29.0%	
Maxine Holloway	*Gre*	258	7.6%	

May 1991				*No change*
3. David Howarth (R)	*LDm*	1565	50.3%	*LDm maj 635 (20.4%)*
Richard Baty	*Con*	930	29.9%	
Kevin Price	*Lab*	616	19.8%	

May 1992				*LDm gain from Con*
1. John Hipkin	*LDm*	1333	47.0%	*LDm maj 312 (11.0%)*
Simon Mitton	*Con*	1021	36.0%	
Simon Gosnell	*Lab*	485	17.1%	

May 1994				*No change*
2. Alan Charlesworth (R)	*LDm*	1597	53.5%	*LDm maj 858 (28.8%) Ind 1996*
Angela Smith	*Lab*	739	24.8%	
Jacqueline Mitton	*Con*	647	21.7%	

May 1995				*No change*
3. David Howarth (R)	*LDm*	1426	54.1%	*LDm maj 736 (27.9%)*
Robert Smith	*Lab*	690	26.2%	
Adam Nichols	*Con*	402	15.3%	
Lydia Howitt	*Gre*	118	4.5%	

May 1996				*No change*
1. John Hipkin (R)	*LDm*	1421	55.8%	*LDm maj 737 (28.9%)*
Robert Smith	*Lab*	684	26.9%	
Jacqueline Mitton	*Con*	441	17.3%	

Castle (contd.)

May 1998				*LDm gain from Ind (see 1994)*
2. J.David White	*LDm*	1172	60.4%	*LDm maj 807 (41.6%)*
Stephen Hartley	*Lab*	365	18.8%	
Richard Hoile	*Con*	293	15.1%	
Marion Barber	*Gre*	112	5.8%	

May 1999				*No change*
3. David Howarth (R)	*LDm*	1459	72.2%	*LDm maj 1139 (56.3%)*
Stephen Hartley	*Lab*	320	15.8%	
James Strachan	*Con*	243	12.0%	

May 2000				*No change*
1. John Hipkin (R)	*LDm*	1195	62.3%	*LDm maj 871 (45.4%)*
Mark J. Taylor	*Con*	324	16.9%	
Denstone Kemp	*Lab*	261	13.6%	
Margaret Wright	*Gre*	137	7.1%	

May 2002				*No change*
2. J.David White (R)	*LDm*	1121	51.4%	*LDm maj 663 (30.4%)*
Rhona Boorman	*Con*	458	21.0%	
Gillian Richardson	*Lab*	412	18.9%	
Stephen Lawrence	*Gre*	188	8.6%	

May 2003				*No change*
3. David Howarth (R)	*LDm*	1226	58.2%	*LDm maj 781 (37.1%)*
Rhona Boorman	*Con*	445	21.1%	
Gillian Richardson	*Lab*	271	12.9%	
Stephen Lawrence	*Gre*	163	7.7%	

General re-warding: Castle gained 6 colleges from Newnham and lost the area eastward from Histon Road to Arbury.

June 2004 (All up elections – 3 vacancies)				*3 LDm*
2. Marie-Louise Holland	*LDm*	1130	51.9%	*Ind from 2007*
1. John Hipkin (R)	*LDm*	1112	51.1%	*Ind from 2007*
3. Simon Kightley	*LDm*	1011	46.4%	*LDm maj 524 (24.1%)*
Jacqueline Mitton	*Con*	487	22.4%	
Janet Webb	*Con*	459	21.1%	
Stephen Lawrence	*Gre*	436	20.0%	
Charles Pilkington	*Con*	434	19.9%	
Jane Jacks	*Lab*	403	18.5%	
Christopher Hemming	*Lab*	320	14.7%	
Duncan Rayner	*Lab*	272	12.5%	

May 2006				*No change*
3. Simon Kightley (R)	*LDm*	985	48.3%	*LDm maj 509 (24.9%)*
Edward MacNaghten	*Con*	476	23.3%	
Stephen Lawrence	*Gre*	298	14.6%	
Lucy Sheerman	*Lab*	282	13.8%	

May 2007				*LDm gain from Ind (see 2004)*
1. Tania Zmura	*LDm*	806	42.5%	*LDm maj 316 (16.6%)*
Edward MacNaghten	*Con*	490	25.8%	
Stephen Lawrence	*Gre*	309	16.3%	
Margery Abbott	*Lab*	293	15.4%	

May 2008				*No change*
2. John Hipkin	*Ind*	851	39.0%	*Ind maj (144 6.6%)*
Valerie Holt	*LDm*	707	32.4%	
Edward MacNaghten	*Con*	255	11.7%	
Samuel Wakeford	*Lab*	225	10.3%	
Stephen Lawrence	*Gre*	145	6.6%	

May 2010				*No change*
3. Simon Kightley (R)	*LDm*	1857	44.7%	*LDm maj 951 (22.9%)*
Warren Clegg	*Con*	906	21.8%	
James Kennedy	*Gre*	749	18.0%	
John Buckingham	*Lab*	641	15.4%	

May 2011				*No change*
1. Philip Tucker	*LDm*	973	33.6%	*LDm maj 245 (8.5%)*
Ashley Walsh	*Lab*	728	25.2%	
Philip Salway	*Con*	620	21.4%	
Jack Toye	*Gre*	572	19.8%	

Castle (contd.)

May 2012				*No change*
2. John Hipkin (R)	*Ind*	925	49.5%	*Ind maj 595 (31.9%)*
Ashley Walsh	*Lab*	330	17.7%	
Alan Levy	*LDm*	275	14.7%	
Nikesh Pandit	*Con*	173	9.3%	
Jack Toye	*Gre*	164	8.8%	

May 2014				*Ind gain from LDm*
3. Marie-Louise Holland	*Ind*	737	27.2%	*Ind maj 20 (0.7%)*
Fergus Blair	*LDm*	717	26.5%	
Mark Reader	*Lab*	565	20.9%	
Sandra Billington	*Gre*	409	15.1%	
Tom Byrne	*Con*	281	10.4%	

May 2015				*No change*
1. Valerie Holt	*LDm*	1288	30.4%	*LDm maj 204 (4.8%)*
Patrick Sheil	*Lab*	1084	25.5%	
Simon Mitton	*Con*	951	22.4%	
Martin Bonner	*Gre*	920	21.7%	

May 2016				*No change*
2. John Hipkin (R)	*Ind*	776	37.9%	*Ind maj 214 (10.5%)*
Patrick Sheil	*Lab*	562	27.5%	
Mark Argent	*LDm*	388	19.0%	
Alacia Gent	*Gre*	191	8.8%	
Edward MacNaghten	*Con*	129	9.3%	

May 2018				*LDm gain from Ind*
3. Cheney-Anne Payne	*LDm*	957	40.8%	*LDm maj 25 (1.1%)*
Mark Reader	*Lab*	932	39.8%	
Othman Cole	*Con*	245	10.5%	
Lucas Ruzowitzky	*Gre*	184	7.8%	
Aidan Powlesland	*Lbt*	26	1.1%	

May 2019				*No change*
1. Greg Chadwick	*LDm*	1186	49.9%	*LDm maj 488 (20.5%)*
Isabel Lambourne	*Lab*	698	29.4%	
Matthew Green	*Gre*	332	14.0%	
Oliver Riley	*Con*	160	6.7%	

Castle (contd.)

No elections in 2020 due to Covid-19 pandemic

General re-warding (see map, near end of book)

May 2021 (All up elections – 3 vacancies)				*2 Lab 1 LDm*
1. Sarah Baigent	*Lab*	938	40.2%	
2. Cheney-Anne Payne (R)	*LDm*	854	36.6%	
3. Simon Smith	*Lab*	810	34.7%	*Lab maj 42 (1.8%)*
Caroline Stoddart	*LDm*	768	32.9%	
Michael Franklin	*LDm*	723	31.0%	
Michael Black	*Lab*	675	29.0%	
Simon Baron	*Gre*	482	20.7%	
Amber-Page Moss	*Gre*	474	20.3%	
James Murray-White	*Gre*	323	13.9%	
Paul Fray	*Con*	241	10.3%	
Mike Halpin	*Con*	241	10.3%	
Philip Salway	*Con*	225	9.7%	
May 2022				*No change*
3. Simon Smith (R)	*Lab*	886	41.8%	*Lab maj 135 (6.4%)*
Caroline Stoddart	*LDm*	751	35.5%	
James Murray-White	*Gre*	370	17.5%	
James Appiah	*Con*	111	5.2%	
May 2023 - 2 vacancies				*No change*
2. Cheney Payne (R)	*LDm*	816	39.1%	
1. Antoinette Nestor	*Lab*	716	34.3%	*Lab maj 84 (4%)*
Mary Murphy	*Lab*	651	31.2%	
David Summerfield	*Ind*	632	30.3%	
Will Tilbrook	*LDm*	437	20.9%	
Esme Hennessy	*Gre*	338	16.2%	
Dan Kittmer	*Gre*	225	10.8%	
Rhona Boorman	*Con*	162	7.8%	
Tomasz Dyl	*Con*	145	6.9%	
May 2024				*No change*
1.Antoinette Nestor (R)	*Lab*	771	40.0%	*Lab maj 364 (18.9%)*
David Summerfield	*Ind*	407	21.1%	
Caroline Stoddart	*LDm*	369	19.1%	
Esmé Hennessy	*Gre*	294	15.2%	
Szymon Sawicki	*Con*	88	4.6%	

Castle (contd.)

May 2026				*Gre gain*
Alex Sage	*Gre*	757	32.2%	*Gre maj 24 (1.0%)*
Luke Paterson	*LDm*	733	31.2%	
Simon Smith (R)	*Lab*	599	25.5%	
Carol Bedson	*Rfm*	115	4.9%	
Dace Ruklisa	*Con*	85	3.6%	
Khalid Abu-Tayyem	*Ind*	64	2.7%	

~~~ **Cherry Hinton** ~~~

November 1935   (All up elections - 3 vacancies)   *Ind, Lab, Ind*

1. Lucy Cooke	*Ind*	379	50.5%	
3. James Fell	*Lab*	374	49.7%	
2. Arthur Doggett	*Ind*	356	47.3%	*Ind maj 6 (0.8%)*
Mabel Fell	*Lab*	350	46.5%	
William Street	*Lab*	320	42.6%	
William Hardesty	*Ind*	260	34.6%	

November 1936   *Lab gain from Ind*

2. Mabel Fell	*Lab*	402	50.4%	*Lab maj 6 (0.8%)*
Arthur Doggett (R)	*Ind*	396	49.6%	

November 1937   *Ind gain from Lab*

3. Arthur Doggett	*Ind*	455	51.1%	*Ind maj 20 (2.2%)*
James Fell (R)	*Lab*	435	48.9%	

November 1938   *Lab gain from Ind*

1. Freda Hardman	*Lab*	515	51.4%	*Lab maj 29 (2.9%)*
Lucy Cooke (R)	*Ind*	486	48.6%	

No elections held during World War II. Elsie Patterson co-opted.

November 1945 (2 vacancies)   *No change*

2. Elsie Patterson (R)	*Lab*	796	58.9%	
1. Edward Burgess	*Lab*	769	56.9%	*Lab maj 3 (0.2%)*
Kelsey Kerridge	*Con*	766	56.7%	
Harold Widdows	*RPA*	370	27.4%	

November 1946   *Con gain from Ind*

3. Donald Denton-Smith	*Con*	847	53.0%	*Con maj 95 (5.9%)*
Violet Taylor	*Lab*	752	47.0%	

November 1947   *Con gain from Lab*

1. Ronald Hearn	*Con*	1153	60.7%	*Con maj 408 (21.5%)*
Edward Burgess (R)	*Lab*	745	39.3%	

May 1949   *Con gain from Lab*

2. Kelsey Kerridge (R)	*Con*	1110	54.7%	*Con maj 191 (9.4%)* (R) Coleridge
Elsie Patterson (R)	*Lab*	919	45.3%	

Cherry Hinton (contd.)

May 1950   *No change*

3. Walter Points	*Con*	1145	58.7%	*Con maj 338 (17.3%)*
Harold Bowles	*Lab*	807	41.3%	

May 1951   *No change*

1. Donald Denton-Smith	*Con*	unopposed

May 1952   *No change*

2. Kelsey Kerridge (R)	*Con*	1354	50.4%	*Con maj 24 (0.9%)*
Senley Melbourne	*Lab*	1330	49.6%	

May 1953   *No change*

3. Walter Points (R)	*Con*	1346	50.1%	*Con maj 7 (0.3%)*
John Clark	*Lab*	1339	49.9%	

May 1954   *Lab gain from Con*

1. Stanley Ambrose	*Lab*	1612	53.2%	*Lab maj 195 (6.4%)*
Herbert Finbow	*Con*	1417	46.8%	

May 1955   *No change*

2. Kelsey Kerridge (R)	*Con*	1677	52.1%	*Con maj 134 (4.2%)*
Stanley Edwards	*Lab*	1543	47.9%	

May 1956   *Lab gain from Con*

3. Stanley Edwards	*Lab*	2117	60.9%	*Lab maj 759 (21.8%)*
Walter Points (R)	*Con*	1358	39.1%	

May 1957   *No change*

1. Richard Reilly	*Lab*	1944	56.6%	*Lab maj 456 (13.3%)*
Ernle Money	*Con*	1488	43.4%	

May 1958   *Lab gain from Con*

2. James Curley	*Lab*	unopposed

January 1959 (byelection)   *Con gain from Lab*

2. Frank Hall	*Con*	995	50.3%	*Con maj 12 (0.6%)*
John Clark	*Lab*	983	49.7%	

May 1959   *No change*

3. Stanley Edwards (R)	*Lab*	1635	43.7%	*Lab maj 78 (2.1%)*
Walter Stubbings	*Con*	1557	41.6%	
Fraser White	*Lib*	552	14.7%	

<h1 style="text-align:center">Cherry Hinton (contd.)</h1>

May 1960				*Lab gain from Con*
1. Richard Reilly (R)	*Lab*	1474	40.5%	*Lab maj 111 (3.1%)*
Walter Stubbings	*Con*	1363	37.4%	
Fraser White	*Lib*	803	22.1%	

May 1961				*Lib gain from Con*
2. Kenneth Johnston	*Lib*	1865	56.4%	*Lib maj 421 (12.7%)*
Leslie McRoberts	*Lab*	1444	43.6%	

May 1962				*Lib gain from Lab*
3. Peter Lowings	*Lib*	1644	55.6%	*Lib maj 330 (11.2%)*
Stanley Edwards (R)	*Lab*	1314	44.4%	

May 1963				*No change*
1. Richard Reilly (R)	*Lab*	2018	50.5%	*Lab maj 38 (1.0%)*
William Rust	*Lib*	1980	49.5%	

May 1964				*Lab gain from Lib*
2. Paul Rayment	*Lab*	2062	50.6%	*Lab maj 51 (1.3%)*
William Rust	*Lib*	2011	49.4%	

May 1965				*No change*
3. Antonia Knowlson	*Lib*	2068	55.8%	*Lib maj 429 (11.6%)*
Gerald Steele	*Lab*	1639	44.2%	

May 1966 (2 vacancies)				*No change*
1. Richard Reilly (R)	*Lab*	1899	45.8%	
2. Gerald Steele	*Lab*	1790	43.1%	*Lab maj 191 (4.6%)*
Derek Bliss	*Con*	1599	38.5%	
John Carlton	*Con*	1444	34.8%	
David Croghan	*Lib*	931	22.4%	
Eric Hands	*Lib*	636	15.3%	

May 1967				*No change*
2. Gerald Steele (R)	*Lab*	1630	42.4%	*Lab maj 127 (3.3%)*
Ronald Wells	*Con*	1503	39.1%	
Joseph Fisher	*Lib*	710	18.5%	

General re-warding: Cherry Hinto's northern boundary changed,

<h1 style="text-align:center">Cherry Hinton (contd.)</h1>

May 1968   *Con gain from Lib*

3. Stanley Allin	*Con*	1823	50.9%	*Con maj 902 (25.2%)*
Frederick Chandler	*Lab*	921	25.7%	
Moira Steel	*Lib*	837	23.4%	

October 1968 (byelection)   *Con gain from Lab*

2. Donald Maltby	*Con*	1466	45.0%	*Con maj 173 (5.3%)*
Leonard Freeman	*Lab*	1293	39.7%	
Moira Steel	*Lib*	500	15.3%	

May 1969   *Con gain from Lab*

1. A.James Johnson	*Con*	2064	63.4%	*Con maj 872 (26.8%)*
Richard Reilly (R)	*ILP*	1192	36.6%	

May 1970   *No change*

2. Donald Maltby (R)	*Con*	2027	54.5%	*Con maj 335 (9.0%)*
Richard Reilly	*Lab*	1692	45.5%	

May 1971   *Lab gain from Con*

3. Richard Reilly	*Lab*	2366	55.7%	*Lab maj 483 (11.4%)*
Stanley Allin (R)	*Con*	1883	44.3%	

May 1972   *Lab gain from Con*

1. Terence Sweeney	*Lab*	2142	51.6%	*Lab maj 135 (3.3%)*
A.James Johnson (R)	*Con*	2007	48.4%	

June 1973 (All up elections - 5 vacancies, all retiring 1976)   *5 Lab*

Terence Sweeney (R)	*Lab*	1961	59.0%	
Julie Carter	*Lab*	1935	58.2%	
Anthony Carter	*Lab*	1894	56.9%	
John N. Hughes	*Lab*	1892	56.9%	(R) Abbey
George Rowling	*Lab*	1685	50.7%	*Lab maj 35 (1.1%)*
A.James Johnson	*Con*	1650	49.6%	
Sylvia Dolby	*Con*	1648	49.5%	
Stanley Allin	*Con*	1647	49.5%	
William Neale	*Con*	1585	47.7%	
Richard Reilly R	*ILP*	734	22.1%	

Cherry Hinton (contd.)

October 1975 (byelection)				*Con gain from Lab*
3. Elizabeth Hodder	*Con*	1467	44.3%	*Con maj 744 (22.5%)*
Stephen Dartford	*Lab*	723	21.8%	
U.Ann Corsellis	*Lib*	505	15.3%	
Charles Spencer	*Ind*	360	10.9%	
Richard Reilly	*Ind*	255	7.7%	

General re-warding: Western parts of Cherry Hinton were transferred to Coleridge and the new Queen Edith's Ward.

May 1976 (All up elections - 3 vacancies)				*3 Con*
2. John Phillips	*Con*	1192	50.8%	
1. John West	*Con*	1086	46.3%	
3. Gerald Coteman	*Con*	1017	43.3%	*Con maj 52 (2.2%)*
Paul Holmes	*Lab*	965	41.1%	
John N. Hughes (R)	*Lab*	932	39.7%	
Stephen Dartford	*Lab*	889	37.9%	

May 1978				*No change*
3. Colin Barker	*Con*	1321	52.0%	*Con maj 104 (4.1%)*
Anthony Carter	*Lab*	1217	48.0%	

May 1979				*Lab gain from Con*
1. Christopher Howard	*Lab*	1804	44.2%	*Lab maj 121 (3.0%)*
John West (R)	*Con*	1683	41.3%	
Charles Burch	*Lib*	591	14.5%	

May 1980				*Lab gain from Con*
2. John Woodhouse	*Lab*	1382	52.6%	*Lab maj 323 (12.3%)*
John Phillips (R)	*Con*	1059	40.3%	
U.Ann Corsellis	*Lib*	187	7.1%	

May 1982				*Lab gain from Con*
3. Adrian Herbert	*Lab*	1123	38.9%	*Lab maj 171 (5.9%)*
Allen Alderson	*Con*	952	33.0%	
Margaret Reiss	*SDP*	809	28.1%	(R) Market

May 1983				*No change*
1. Christopher Howard (R)	*Lab*	1443	46.0%	*Lab maj 454 (14.5%)*
Kevin Akehurst	*Con*	989	31.5%	
Gale Waller	*Lib*	703	22.4%	

Cherry Hinton (contd.)

May 1984				*No change*
2. John Woodhouse (R)	*Lab*	1389	49.1%	*Lab maj 543 (19.2%)*
Rowena Davies	*Con*	846	29.9%	
June Greenwell	*SDP*	592	20.9%	

May 1986				*No change*
3. Thomas Ling	*Lab*	1199	41.8%	*Lab maj 263 (9.2%)*
Ann Wright	*Con*	936	32.6%	
Norman Braddick	*SDP*	734	25.6%	

May 1987				*Con gain from Lab*
1. Ann Wright	*Con*	1262	37.3%	*Con maj 62 (1.8%)*
Christopher Howard (R)	*Lab*	1200	35.5%	
Mary Basham	*Lib*	918	27.2%	

May 1988				*No change*
2. John Woodhouse (R)	*Lab*	1623	51.6%	*Lab maj 432 (13.7%)*
Barry Wright	*Con*	1191	37.8%	
H.Michael Allan	*SLD*	333	10.6%	

May 1990				*No change*
3. Alexander MacEachern	*Lab*	1502	53.9%	*Lab maj 617 (22.1%)*
Richard Baty	*Con*	885	31.7%	
Patrick Tooth	*Gre*	218	7.8%	
Ken Lowe	*LDm*	184	6.6%	

May 1991				*No change*
1. Stephen Hillier	*Con*	1182	44.4%	*Con maj 32 (1.2%)*
Anthony Schofield	*Lab*	1150	43.2%	
Kevin Wilkins	*LDm*	332	12.5%	

May 1992				*Con gain from Lab*
2. M.Tim Seaton	*Con*	1193	43.6%	*Con maj 220 (8.1%)*
Anthony Schofield	*Lab*	973	35.5%	
Suzanne Henney	*LDm*	220	8.0%	
Elizabeth Cooper	*Gre*	66	2.4%	
Peter Chaplin	*USp*	65	2.4%	

May 1994				*No change*
3. Alexander MacEachern (R)	*Lab*	1391	52.5%	*Lab maj 503 (19.0%)*
Jason Webb	*Con*	888	33.5%	
Ashley Woodford	*LDm*	370	14.0%	

<h1 style="text-align:center">Cherry Hinton (contd.)</h1>

May 1995   *Lab gain from Con*

1. Robert Dryden	*Lab*	1478	63.3%	*Lab maj 876 (37.5%)*
Eric Barrett-Payton	*Con*	602	25.8%	
Ashley Woodford	*LDm*	256	11.0%	

May 1996   *Lab gain from Con*

2. Geoffrey Howe	*Lab*	1022	55.4%	*Lab maj 512 (27.8%)*
Eric Barrett-Payton	*Con*	510	27.6%	
Edna Howarth	*LDm*	313	17.0%	

May 1998   *Con gain from Lab*

3. Graham Stuart	*Con*	893	46.6%	*Con maj 31 (1.6%)*
Richard Carling	*Lab*	862	45.0%	
Ashley Woodford	*LDm*	161	8.4%	

May 1999   *No change*

Robert Dryden (R)	*Lab*	1264	53.0%	*Lab maj 275 (11.5%)*
Christopher Howell	*Con*	989	41.4%	
Frances Amrani	*LDm*	134	5.6%	

May 2000   *Con gain from Lab*

Christopher Howell	*Con*	1138	49.8%	*Con maj 144 (6.3%)*
George Rowling	*Lab*	994	43.5%	
Frances Amrani	*LDm*	152	6.7%	

May 2002   *No change*

Graham Stuart (R)	*Con*	1174	49.3%	*Con maj 226 (9.5%)*
Stuart Newbold	*Lab*	948	39.8%	
Frances Amrani	*LDm*	196	8.2%	
Daryl Tayar	*Gre*	64	2.7%	

May 2003   *No change*

1. Robert Dryden (R)	*Lab*	1072	43.3%	*Lab maj 51 (2.1%)*
Justin Hinchcliffe	*Con*	1021	41.2%	
Geoffrey Heathcock	*LDm*	311	12.6%	
Shayne Mitchell	*Gre*	73	2.9%	

General re-warding: Cherry Hinton gained areas in the west from Coleridge and Queen Edith's.

Cherry Hinton (contd.)

3. Robert Dryden (R)	*Lab*	1275	43.8%	
2. Russell McPherson	*Lab*	1057	36.3%	
1. Eric Barrett-Payton	*Con*	1027	35.3%	*Con maj 89 (3.1%)*
Christopher Howell (R)	*Con*	1014	34.8%	
Graham Palmer	*Con*	983	33.8%	
Stuart Newbold	*Lab*	938	32.2%	
Geoffrey Heathcock	*LDm*	556	19.1%	
Ben Hutchings	*LDm*	400	13.7%	
Simon Rodgers	*LDm*	350	12.0%	
Neil Ford	*Gre*	242	8.3%	

May 2006   *Lab gain from Con*

1. Stuart Newbold	*Lab*	1071	42.9%	*Lab maj 207 (8.3%)*
Eric Barrett-Payton (R)	*Con*	864	34.6%	
Natalie Mayer-Hutchings	*LDm*	367	14.7%	
Neil Ford	*Gre*	193	7.7%	

May 2007   *No change*

2. Russell McPherson (R)	*Lab*	1126	46.1%	*Lab maj 320 (13.1%)*
Sarah El-Neil	*Con*	806	33.0%	
L.Keith Edkins	*LDm*	257	10.5%	
Hamish Downer	*Gre*	130	5.3%	
Marjorie Barr	*UKIP*	121	5.0%	

May 2008   *No change*

3. Robert Dryden (R)	*Lab*	1247	52.0%	*Lab maj 420 (17.5%)*
Sarah El-Neil	*Con*	827	34.5%	
David Willingham	*LDm*	167	7.0%	
Neil Ford	*Gre*	157	6.5%	

May 2010   *No change*

1. Stuart Newbold (R)	*Lab*	1610	38.4%	*Lab maj 379 (9.0%)*
Edward Macnaghten	*Con*	1231	29.4%	
L.Keith Edkins	*LDm*	1023	24.4%	
Ross Pooley	*Gre*	328	7.8%	

Cherry Hinton (contd.)

May 2011 (2 vacancies)				*No change*
2. Mark Ashton	*Lab*	1525	51.5%	
1. Russell McPherson (R)	*Lab*	1464	49.4%	*Lab maj 584 (19.7%)*
Edward Turnham	*Con*	880	29.7%	
Timothy Haire	*Con*	865	29.2%	
Jane Esgate	*Gre*	304	10.3%	
Neil Ford	*Gre*	267	9.0%	
L.Keith Edkins	*LDm*	246	8.3%	
Joe Ryan	*LDm*	205	6.9%	

May 2012				*No change*
3. Robert Dryden (R)	*Lab*	1556	73.2%	*Lab maj 1171 (55.1%)*
Angela Ozturk	*Con*	385	18.1%	
L.Keith Edkins	*LDm*	185	8.7%	

May 2014				*No change*
1. Russell McPherson (R)	*Lab*	1533	60.6%	*Lab maj 920 (36.4%)*
Timothy Haire	*Con*	613	24.2%	
L.Keith Edkins	*LDm*	383	15.1%	

May 2015				*No change*
2. Mark Ashton (R)	*Lab*	1839	43.5%	*Lab maj 996 (23.6%)*
Timothy Haire	*Con*	843	19.9%	
Ed Sexton	*LDm*	790	18.7%	
Alex Crowson	*UKIP*	393	9.3%	
Phillip Barnett	*Gre*	364	8.6%	

May 2016				*No change*
3. Robert Dryden (R)	*Lab*	1373	60.8%	*Lab maj 1006 (44.5%)*
Eric Barrett-Payton	*Con*	367	16.2%	
Jamie Dalzell	*LDm*	210	9.3%	
Richard Jeffs	*UKIP*	166	7.3%	
Caitlin Patterson	*Gre*	143	6.3%	

May 2018				*No change*
1.Russell McPherson (R)	*Lab*	1282	56.8%	*Lab maj 841 (37.2%)*
Eric Barrett-Payton	*Con*	441	19.5%	
John Oakes	*LDm*	364	16.1%	
Jenny Richens	*Gre*	171	7.6%	

May 2019   *No change*
1. Mark Ashton (R)   *Lab*   1062   49.4%   *Lab maj 598 (27.8%)*
Henry Wright   *LDm*   464   21.6%
Jennifer Richens   *Gre*   352   16.4%
Mohammed Hossain   *Con*   270   12.6%

No elections in 2020 due to Covid-19 pandemic

General re-warding (see map, near end of book)

May 2021 (All up elections – 3 vacancies)   *3 Lab*
1. Mark Ashton (R)   *Lab*   1354   53.1%
2. Robert Dryden (R)   *Lab*   1235   48.4%
3. Russell McPherson (R)*Lab*   1235   48.4%   *Lab maj 694 (27.2%)*
Eric Barrett-Payton   *Con*   541   21.2%
David Smith   *Con*   453   17.8%
James Hill   *LDm*   387   15.2%
Richard Potter   *Gre*   357   14.0%
Eli Langfere   *Gre*   333   13.1%
Caitlin Patterson   *Gre*   315   12.4%
Delowar Hossain   *Con*   280   11.0%
Archie McCann   *LDm*   241   9.5%
Freddie Poser   *LDm*   215   8.4%

May 2022   *No change*
3. Russell McPherson (R)*Lab*   1345   58.3%   *Lab maj 954 (41.3%)*
Eric Barrett-Payton   *Con*   391   16.9%
Richard Potter   *Gre*   290   12.6%
Peter McLaughlin   *LDm*   283   12.3%

May 2023   *No change*
2. Robert Dryden (R)   *Lab*   1119   43.0%   *Lab maj 63 (2.4%)*
Zachary Marsh   *Con*   1056   40.6%
Richard Potter   *Gre*   235   9.0%
Archie McCann   *LDm*   193   7.4%

May 2024   *No change*
1.Mark Ashton (R)   *Lab*   1149   48.5%   *Lab maj 514 (21.7%)*
Mo Pantall   *Con*   635   26.8%
Aiden Roe   *LDm*   356   15.0%
Josh Morris-Blake   *Gre*   228   9.6%

May 2026   *No change*

Russ McPherson (R)	*Lab*	864	30.9%	Lab maj 133 (4.8%)
Anusha Iyer	*Gre*	731	26.2%	
Mike Nicholson	*Rfm*	484	17.3%	
Ahmad Rushdhi	*LDm*	399	14.3%	
Eric Barrett-Payton	*Con*	315	11.3%	

~~~ **Coleridge** ~~~

November 1935 (All up elections - 3 vacancies)   *3 Con*
2. Harry Ambrose	*Con*	1249	65.1%	*(R) Cambridge Without*
1. Donald Stevenson	*Con*	1056	55.0%	
3. George Wilding	*Con*	1018	53.0%	*Con maj 220 (11.5%)*
David Hardman	*Lab*	798	41.6%	
Colin Clarke	*Lab*	696	36.3%	
James Phillips	*Lab*	619	32.3%	

December 1935 (byelection)   *No change*
2. Frederick Kay	*Con*	678	52.1%	*Con maj 55 (4.2%)*
Frederick Hutt	*Lab*	623	47.9%	

November 1936   *No change*
3. George Wilding (R)	*Con*	1000	59.7%	*Con maj 325 (19.4%)*
Colin Clarke	*Lab*	675	40.3%	

November 1937   *No change*
1. Donald Stevenson (R)	*Con*	831	60.2%	*Con maj 282 (20.4%)*
James Phillips	*Lab*	549	39.8%	

November 1938   *No change*
2. Frederick Kay (R)	*Con*	1066	53.3%	*Con maj (131 6.5%)*
Harry Clover	*Lab*	935	46.7%	

No elections held during World War II.

November 1945   *No change*
3. George Wilding (R)	*Con*	1616	54.2%	*Con maj 251 (8.4%)*
Frank Turvill	*Lab*	1365	45.8%	

December 1945 (byelection)   *No change*
1. Kelsey Kerridge	*Con*	1787	57.8%	*Con maj 481 (15.6%)*
Frank Turvill	*Lab*	1306	42.2%	

November 1946   *No change*
2. Harold Ridgeon	*Con*	2002	61.2%	*Con maj 731 (22.3%)*
Pauline French	*Lab*	1271	38.8%	

November 1947   *No change*
3. Alfred Gibbs	*Con*	2470	65.2%	*Con maj 1153 (30.4%)*
John Saunders	*Lab*	1317	34.8%	

<h1 style="text-align:center">Coleridge (contd.)</h1>

May 1949 — *No change*

1. Wallace Cole	*Con*	2222	64.8%	*Con maj 1013 (29.5%)*
John Saunders	*Lab*	1209	35.2%	

May 1950 — *No change*

2. Harold Ridgeon (R)	*Con*	unopposed	

May 1951 — *No change*

3. Cyril Bailey	*Con*	unopposed	

May 1952 — *No change*

1. Wallace Cole (R)	*Con*	2165	58.3%	*Con maj 614 (16.5%)*
John Clark	*Lab*	1551	41.7%	

May 1953 — *No change*

2. Harold Ridgeon (R)	*Con*	2114	65.7%	*Con maj 1010 (31.4%)*
Edward Ellis	*Lab*	1104	34.3%	

May 1954 — *No change*

3. Cyril Bailey (R)	*Con*	unopposed	

May 1955 (2 vacancies) — *No change*

1. Gladys Burn	*Con*	unopposed	
2. Wallace Cole (R)	*Con*	unopposed	

(Order determined by lot)

November 1955 (byelection) — *No change*

3. Herbert Finbow	*Con*	unopposed	

May 1956 — *No change*

2. Wallace Cole (R)	*Con*	1590	58.2%	*Con maj 446 (16.3%)*
Richard Reilly	*Lab*	1144	41.8%	

May 1957 — *No change*

3. Herbert Finbow (R)	*Con*	1617	53.0%	*Con maj 184 (6.0%)*
John Clark	*Lab*	1433	47.0%	

May 1958 — *No change*

1. Gladys Burn (R)	*Con*	1892	58.8%	*Con maj 568 (17.7%)*
Basil Bord	*Lab*	1324	41.2%	

Coleridge (contd.)

May 1959				*No change*
2. Wallace Cole (R)	*Con*	1686	78.7%	*Con maj 1231 (57.5%)*
Leslie McRoberts	*ILP*	455	21.3%	

May 1960				*No change*
3. Herbert Finbow (R)	*Con*	1474	63.1%	*Con maj 613 (26.3%)*
Josef Schicker	*Lab*	861	36.9%	

May 1961			*No change*
1. Gladys Burn (R)	*Con*	unopposed	

May 1962				*No change*
2. Wallace Cole (R)	*Con*	1313	60.6%	*Con maj 460 (21.2%)*
Leslie McRoberts	*Lab*	853	39.4%	

May 1963				*No change*
3. Herbert Finbow (R)	*Con*	1370	50.8%	*Con maj 45 (1.7%)*
Damaris Parker-Rhodes	*Lab*	1325	49.2%	

May 1964				*No change*
1. Gladys Burn (R)	*Con*	1716	54.8%	*Con maj 298 (9.5%)*
Damaris Parker-Rhodes	*Lab*	1418	45.2%	

May 1965				*No change*
2. Bernard Sargent	*Con*	1802	63.8%	*Con maj 780 (27.6%)*
Richard Pryke	*Lab*	1022	36.2%	

May 1966				*No change*
3. Herbert Finbow (R)	*Con*	1770	54.7%	*Con maj 305 (9.4%)*
Stanley Edwards	*Lab*	1465	45.3%	

May 1967				*No change*
1. Gladys Burn (R)	*Con*	1639	62.5%	*Con maj 656 (25.0%)*
Stanley Edwards	*Lab*	983	37.5%	

July 1967 (byelection)			*No change*
3. Donald Mackay	*Con*	unopposed	

General re-warding: Coleridge not affected

Coleridge (contd.)

May 1968   *No change*
2. Bernard Sargent (R)   *Con*   1620   75.2%   *Con maj 1085 (50.3%)*
Damaris Parker-Rhodes   *Lab*   535   24.8%

May 1969   *No change*
3. Donald Mackay (R)   *Con*   1840   66.7%   *Con maj 922 (33.4%)*
Hugh Percival   *Lab*   918   33.3%

May 1970   *No change*
1. Ivie Pickett   *Con*   1593   60.8%   *Con maj 565 (21.6%)*
Hugh Percival   *Lab*   1028   39.2%

September 1970 (byelection)   *No change*
2. Elizabeth Wylie-Croker *Con*   885   51.8%   *Con maj 61 (3.6%)*
Hugh Percival   *Lab*   824   48.2%

May 1971   *Lab gain from Con*
2. Hugh Percival   *Lab*   1515   52.7%   *Lab maj 154 (5.4%)*
Elizabeth Wylie-Croker (R) *Con*   1361   47.3%

May 1972   *No change*
3. Donald Mackay (R)   *Con*   1555   53.9%   *Con maj 223 (7.8%)*
Helen Grant   *Lab*   1332   46.1%

June 1973 (All up elections - 4 vacancies, all retiring 1976)   *Lib, Lab, 2 Con*
M.Joan Fitch   *Lib*   1207   43.2%
Hugh Percival (R)   *Lab*   1107   39.6%
Gladys Burn (R)   *Con*   1053   37.7%
Donald Mackay (R)   *Con*   1031   36.9%   *Con maj 124 (4.4%)*
Douglas Anderson   *Con*   923   33.0%
Damaris Parker-Rhodes   *Lab*   907   32.5%
Kathleen Hartley   *Lab*   891   31.9%
Graham Knowles   *Con*   863   30.9%
Meike Champernowne   *Lab*   843   30.2%
Carol Farman   *Lib*   813   29.1%
Eric Hands   *Lib*   796   28.5%
L.Keith Edkins   *Lib*   743   26.6%

General re-warding: Coleridge lost the area south of Cherry Hinton Road; gained that around Birdwood Road, and swapped areas near Mill Road with Romsey.

Coleridge (contd.)

May 1976 (All up elections - 3 vacancies)   *3 Con*

1. Donald Mackay (R)	*Con*	1067	44.0%	
3. Frederick Burling	*Con*	1044	43.0%	
2. Douglas Anderson	*Con*	996	41.0%	*Con maj 91 (3.7%)*
Hugh Percival (R)	*Lab*	905	37.3%	
James Curley	*Lab*	819	33.7%	
O.M.Wendy Nicol (R)	*Lab*	808	33.3%	
Alan Hill	*Lib*	329	13.6%	
L.Keith Edkins	*Lib*	288	11.9%	
Chris Townsend	*Lib*	269	11.1%	

 (O.M.Wendy Nicol was retiring councillor for Abbey)

May 1978   *No change*

2. Charles Seagrave	*Con*	979	48.5%	*Con maj 119 (5.9%)*
James Curley	*Lab*	860	42.6%	
Philip Mitchell	*Lib*	178	8.8%	

May 1979   *No change*

3. Frederick Burling (R)	*Con*	1730	45.3%	*Con maj 250 (6.6%)*
Gordon Douglas	*Lab*	1480	38.8%	
Philip Mitchell	*Lib*	606	15.9%	

May 1980   *Lab gain from Con*

1. Mark Todd	*Lab*	1236	49.0%	*Lab maj 238 (9.4%)*
Donald Mackay (R)	*Con*	998	39.5%	
Geoffrey Heathcock	*Lib*	291	11.5%	

May 1982   *No change*

2. Charles Seagrave (R)	*Con*	1127	41.3%	*Con maj 124 (4.5%)*
Eleanor Fairclough	*Lab*	1003	36.8%	
Stephen Hunter	*Lib*	598	21.9%	

May 1983   *No change*

3. Frederick Burling (R)	*Con*	1334	44.2%	*Con maj 29 (1.0%)*
Anthony Carter	*Lab*	1305	43.2%	
Stephen Hunter	*Lib*	379	12.6%	

May 1984   *No change*

1. Mark Todd (R)	*Lab*	1538	48.7%	*Lab maj 283 (9.0%)*
Ian Cornwell	*Con*	1255	39.7%	
Simon Lavery	*Lib*	367	11.6%	

Coleridge (contd.)

May 1986				*Lab gain from Con*
2. M.Alison New	*Lab*	1474	48.3%	*Lab maj 290 (9.5%)*
Gordon Beckett	*Con*	1184	38.8%	
Andrew Paton	*Lib*	395	12.9%	

May 1987				*No change*
3. Frederick Burling (R)	*Con*	1559	46.1%	*Con maj 222 (6.6%)*
Martin Blake	*Lab*	1337	39.5%	
Andrew Paton	*Lib*	485	14.3%	

May 1988				*No change*
1. Mark Todd (R)	*Lab*	1807	55.3%	*Lab maj 540 (16.5%)*
Rodney Stokes	*Con*	1267	38.8%	
Catherine Bowden	*SLD*	194	5.9%	

January 1989 (byelection)				*Lab gain from Con*
3. Martin Blake	*Lab*	1331	49.8%	*Lab maj 220 (8.2%)*
Rodney Stokes	*Con*	1111	41.5%	
Catherine Bowden	*SLD*	233	8.7%	

May 1990 (2 vacancies)				*No change*
2. Jessie Ball	*Lab*	1721	54.8%	
3. M.Alison New (R)	*Lab*	1491	47.5%	*Lab maj 502 (16.0%)*
Justin Coleman	*Con*	989	31.5%	
Jean Shinn	*Con*	979	31.2%	
Valerie Mackie	*LDm*	238	7.6%	
Kathryn Robinson	*LDm*	212	6.7%	
Jennifer Belza	*Gre*	193	6.1%	
Gabrielle Hutton	*Gre*	183	5.8%	

May 1991				*No change*
3. I.Paul Diamond	*Lab*	1320	48.2%	*Lab maj 309 (11.3%)*
Audrey Hull	*Con*	1011	37.0%	
Stephen Howarth	*LDm*	290	10.6%	
Yvonne Douglas	*Gre*	115	4.2%	

May 1992				*No change*
1. Jeremy Benstead	*Lab*	1153	46.1%	*Lab maj 44 (1.8%)*
A.Richard Jones	*Con*	1109	44.3%	
Andrew Paton	*LDm*	241	9.6%	

Coleridge (contd.)

May 1994				*No change*
2. E.Ruth Bagnall	*Lab*	1545	61.0%	*Lab maj 938 (37.0%)*
Stephen George	*Con*	607	24.0%	
Andrew Hoddinott	*LDm*	382	15.1%	

May 1995				*No change*
3. Raith Overhill	*Lab*	1260	58.3%	*Lab maj 785 (36.3%)*
Jeremy Froggett	*Con*	475	22.0%	
Tricia Charlesworth	*LDm*	427	19.8%	

May 1996				*No change*
1. Jeremy Benstead (R)	*Lab*	1234	62.1%	*Lab maj 734 (36.9%)*
Pamela Axhorn	*Con*	500	25.2%	
Evelyn Corder	*LDm*	254	12.8%	

May 1998				*No change*
2. E.Ruth Bagnall (R)	*Lab*	873	61.7%	*Lab maj 510 (36.0%)*
Eric Barrett-Payton	*Con*	363	25.6%	
Richard Folley	*LDm*	180	12.7%	

May 1999				*No change*
3. Berni Callaghan	*Lab*	908	60.1%	*Lab maj 544 (36.0%)*
Fiona McNish	*Con*	364	24.1%	
Richard Folley	*LDm*	239	15.8%	

May 2000				*No change*
1. Jeremy Benstead (R)	*Lab*	789	52.6%	*Lab maj 356 (23.7%)*
James Strachan	*Con*	433	28.8%	
Judith Pinnington	*LDm*	279	18.6%	

May 2002				*No change*
2. E.Ruth Bagnall (R)	*Lab*	938	50.6%	*Lab maj 484 (26.1%)*
Martin Hall	*Con*	454	24.5%	
Jonathan Monroe	*LDm*	267	14.4%	
Damian Docherty	*Gre*	94	5.1%	
Albert Watts	*UKIP*	53	2.9%	
Simon Sedgwick-Jell	*SoA*	46	2.5%	

Coleridge (contd.)

May 2003				*No change*
3. Berni Callaghan (R)	*Lab*	742	41.1%	*Lab maj 171 (9.5%)*
Martin Hall	*Con*	571	31.6%	
Laura Doherty	*LDm*	254	14.1%	
Richard Rippin	*Gre*	95	5.3%	
Simon Sedgwick-Jell	*SoA*	74	4.1%	
Albert Watts	*UKIP*	70	3.9%	

General re-warding: Coleridge gained the Homerton St area from Trumpington and the south side of Cherry Hinton Road from Queen Edith's; lost the Walpole Road area to Cherry Hinton and Greville Road and William Smith Close to Romsey.

June 2004 (All up elections – 3 vacancies)				*3 Lab*
2. Berni Callaghan (R)	*Lab*	782	36.4%	
1. Jeremy Benstead (R)	*Lab*	753	35.1%	
3. Lewis Herbert	*Lab*	743	34.6%	*Lab maj 231 (10.8%)*
Edward Macnaghten	*Con*	512	23.9%	
Steven Mastin	*Con*	511	23.8%	
Andrew Blackhurst	*LDm*	490	22.8%	
Rebecca Folley	*LDm*	477	22.2%	
K.Monica Waters	*Con*	469	21.9%	
Thomas Yates	*LDm*	372	17.3%	
James Grinham	*Gre*	340	15.8%	
Albert Watts	*UKIP*	187	8.7%	

July 2005 (byelection)				*No change*
2. Benjamin Stafford	*Lab*	829	46.8%	*Lab maj 191 (10.8%)*
Andrew Blackhurst	*LDm*	638	36.0%	
Steven Mastin	*Con*	263	14.8%	
Albert Watts	*UKIP*	42	2.4%	

May 2006				*No change*
3. Lewis Herbert (R)	*Lab*	909	41.8%	*Lab maj 432 (19.9%)*
Andrew Blackhurst	*LDm*	477	22.0%	
Stephen Jones	*Con*	463	21.3%	
Hamish Downer	Gre	186	8.6%	
Albert Watts	*UKIP*	138	6.4%	

Coleridge (contd.)

May 2007 (2 vacancies) *No change*

1. Jeremy Benstead (R)	*Lab*	861	39.9%	
2. Tariq Sadiq	*Lab*	739	34.2%	*Lab maj 18 (0.8%)*
Christopher Howell	*Con*	721	33.4%	
Richard Normington	*Con*	662	30.7%	
Emma Lindsay	*LDm*	312	14.5%	
Valerie Hopkins	*Gre*	253	11.7%	
Thomas Yates	*LDm*	248	11.5%	
Neil Ford	*Gre*	215	10.0%	
Albert Watts	*UKIP*	116	5.4%	

May 2008 *Con gain from Lab*

2. Christopher Howell	*Con*	955	40.2%	*Con maj 14 (0.6%)*
Tariq Sadiq (R)	*Lab*	941	39.7%	
Alain Desmier	*LDm*	219	9.2%	
Valerie Hopkins	*Gre*	193	8.1%	
Albert Watts	*UKIP*	65	2.7%	

May 2010 *No change*

3. Lewis Herbert (R)	*Lab*	1320	32.3%	*Lab maj 160 (3.9%)*
Andrew Bower	*Con*	1160	28.4%	
Thomas Yates	*LDm*	1040	25.5%	
Valerie Hopkins	*Gre*	446	10.9%	
Albert Watts	*UKIP*	118	2.9%	

November 2010 (byelection) *Lab gain from Con*

2. George Owers	*Lab*	900	44.0%	*Lab maj 166 (8.1%)*
Andrew Bower	*Con*	734	35.9%	
Sarah Barnes	*LDm*	223	10.9%	
Valerie Hopkins	*Gre*	137	6.7%	
Albert Watts	*UKIP*	53	2.6%	

May 2011 *No change*

1. Jeremy Benstead (R)	*Lab*	1346	46.9%	*Lab maj 477 (16.6%)*
Andrew Bower	*Con*	869	30.3%	
Valerie Hopkins	*Gre*	368	12.8%	
Thomas Yates	*LDm*	285	9.9%	

Coleridge (contd.)

May 2012 — *No change*

2. George Owers (R)	*Lab*	1228	59.6%	*Lab maj 806 (39.1%)*
Samuel Barker	*Con*	422	20.5%	
Shaun Esgate	*Gre*	228	11.1%	
Thomas Yates	*LDm*	183	8.9%	

May 2014 — *No change*

3. Lewis Herbert (R)	*Lab*	1326	51.6%	*Lab maj 896 (34.9%)*
Samuel Barker	*Con*	430	16.7%	
Donald Adey	*LDm*	368	14.3%	
Shaun Esgate	*Gre*	358	13.9%	
The dragon fairy Puffles	*Ind*	89	3.5%	

May 2015 — *No change*

1. Jeremy Benstead (R)	*Lab*	1606	38.1%	*Lab maj 562 (13.3%)*
Simon Cooper	*LDm*	1044	24.8%	
Samuel Barker	*Con*	748	17.7%	
Shaun Esgate	*Gre*	558	13.2%	
Bill Kaminski	*UKIP*	259	6.1%	

May 2016 — *No change*

2. Rosy Moore	*Lab*	1404	60.3%	*Lab maj 1060 (45.6%)*
Samuel Barker	*Con*	344	14.8%	
Raymundo Carlos	*LDm*	234	10.1%	
Virgil Ierubino	*Gre*	187	8.0%	
Bill Kaminski	*UKIP*	158	6.8%	

May 2018 — *No change*

3. Lewis Herbert (R)	*Lab*	1303	55.9%	*Lab maj 893 (38.3%)*
Lindsey Tate	*LDm*	410	17.6%	
Donald Douglas	*Con*	388	16.7%	
Sarah Nicmanis	*Gre*	228	9.8%	

May 2019 — *No change*

1. Grace Hadley	*Lab*	1041	46.0%	*Lab maj 619 (27.4%)*
Alex Harrison	*LDm*	422	18.7%	
Sarah Nicmanis	*Gre*	395	17.5%	
Donald Douglas	*Con*	250	11.1%	
Bill Kaminski	*UKIP*	153	6.8%	

No elections in 2020 due to Covid-19 pandemic

General re-warding (see map, near end of book)

May 2021 (All up elections – 3 vacancies)   · *3 Lab*

1. Lewis Herbert (R)	*Lab*	1289	49.8%	
2. Rosy Moore (R)	*Lab*	1205	46.6%	
3. Anna Smith (R Romsey)	*Lab*	1067	41.2%	*Lab maj 406 (15.7%)*
Bridget Bradshaw	*Gre*	661	25.5%	
Sarah Lightowlers	*Gre*	498	19.2%	
Tim Brunton	*LDm*	384	14.8%	
Robert Nelson	*Con*	383	14.8%	
Gail Kenney	*Con*	376	14.5%	
Iain Webb	*Gre*	364	14.1%	
Peter McLaughlin	*LDm*	331	12.8%	
Linda Yeatman	*Con*	321	12.4%	
Freddie Frisk	*LDm*	287	11.1%	

May 2022   *No change*

3. Anna Smith (R)	*Lab*	1363	56.3%	*Lab maj 948 (39.2%)*
Sarah Nicmanis	*Gre*	415	17.2%	
Robin Nelson	*Con*	338	14.0%	
Sam Oliver	*LDm*	236	9.8%	
Monica Hone	*Ind*	67	2.8%	

May 2023 - 2 vacancies   *No change*

2. Rosy Moore (R)	*Lab*	1085	44.7%	
1. Tim Griffin	*Lab*	895	36.9%	*Lab maj 234 (9.6%)*
Sarah Nicmanis	*Gre*	661	27.2%	
Eric Barrett-Payton	*Con*	627	25.8%	
Robin Nelson	*Con*	611	25.2%	
Peter Price	*Gre*	397	16.4%	
Judy Brunton	*LDm*	259	10.7%	
Tim Brunton	*LDm*	194	8.0%	

May 2024   *No change*

1.Tim Griffin (R)	*Lab*	1124	43.5%	*Lab maj 243 (9.4%)*
Sarah Nicmanis	*Gre*	881	34.1%	
Shapour Meftah	*Con*	419	16.2%	
Judy Brunton	*LDm*	158	6.1%	

Coleridge (contd.)

May 2026   *Gre gain*

Sarah Nicmanis	*Gre*	1150	39.1%	*Gre maj 80 (2.7%)*
Anna Smith (R)	*Lab*	1070	36.4%	
Steve Burdett	*Rfm*	302	10.3%	
Sam Worthington	*Con*	222	7.6%	
Tim Brunton	*LDm*	196	6.7%	

May 2026   *Gre gain*

Sarah Nicmanis	*Gre*	1150	39.1%	*Gre maj 80 (2.7%)*
Anna Smith (R)	*Lab*	1070	36.4%	
Steve Burdett	*Rfm*	302	10.3%	
Sam Worthington	*Con*	222	7.6%	
Tim Brunton	*LDm*	196	6.7%	

~~~ **East Chesterton** ~~~

November 1935 (All up elections - 3 vacancies)   *WCA, Ind, Con*

1. Dorothy Stevenson	*WCA*	1347	55.3%	(R) North Chesterton
3. George Edwards (R)	*Ind*	1247	51.2%	
2. Alexander Eraut (R)	*Con*	881	36.2%	*Con maj 12 (0.5%)*
Marjorie McNair	*Lib*	869	35.7%	
Joseph Holt	*Lab*	739	30.4%	
F.W. Edwards	*Lab*	590	24.2%	

November 1936   *No change*

| **2. Alexander Eraut** (R) | *Con* | 789 | 55.5% | *Con maj 156 (11.0%)* |
| Leonard Doggett | *Lab* | 633 | 44.5% | |

November 1937   *No change*

| **3. George Edwards** (R) | *Ind* | 865 | 71.5% | *Ind maj 520 (43.0%)* |
| Edward Burgess | *Lab* | 345 | 28.5% | |

November 1938   *No change*

| **1. Dorothy Stevenson** (R) | *WCA* | unopposed | | |

January 1939 (byelection)   *Con gain from WCA*

1. Herbert Banham	*Con*	727	42.1%	*Con maj 160 (9.3%)*
Edward Burgess	*Lab*	567	32.9%	
Jeannie Milson Pye	*WCA*	431	25.0%	

No elections held during World War II.

November 1945   *Lab gain from Con*

| **2. Harry Scarlett** | *Lab* | 1433 | 60.1% | *Lab maj 483 (20.3%)* |
| Alexander Eraut (R) | *Con* | 950 | 39.9% | |

November 1946   *No change*

| **3. George Edwards** (R) | *Ind* | 1588 | 55.9% | *Ind maj 334 (11.8%)* |
| Ernest Harding | *Lab* | 1254 | 44.1% | |

November 1947   *No change*

| **1. Herbert Banham** (R) | *Con* | 2243 | 64.8% | *Con maj 1025 (29.6%)* |
| Harold Bowles | *Lab* | 1218 | 35.2% | |

May 1949   *Con gain from Lab*

| **2. John B Collins** | *Con* | 2099 | 59.1% | *Con maj 644 (18.1%)* |
| Ernest Harding | *Lab* | 1455 | 40.9% | |

East Chesterton (contd.)

June 1949 (byelection)				*No change*
1. Cora Banham	*Con*	1339	62.6%	*Con maj 539 (25.2%)*
Ernest Harding	*Lab*	800	37.4%	

May 1950				*No change*
3. George Edwards (R)	*Con*	1784	57.4%	*Con maj 461 (14.8%)*
Robert Fordham	*Lab*	1323	42.6%	

May 1951			*No change*
1. Cora Banham (R)	*Con*	unopposed	

May 1952				*Lab gain from Con*
2. Leonard Wordingham	*Lab*	1522	44.7%	*Lab maj 12 (0.4%)*
John B Collins (R)	*Con*	1510	44.4%	
John O'Hannan	*Ind*	370	10.9%	

May 1953				*Con gain from Lab*
3. Cecilia Traylen	*Con*	1296	41.3%	*Con maj 49 (1.6%)*
Arthur Cobill	*Lab*	1247	39.7%	
George Edwards (R)	*Ind*	598	19.0%	

May 1954				*Lab gain from Con*
1. Robert Davies	*Lab*	1614	51.5%	*Lab maj 94 (3.0%)*
Cora Banham (R)	*Con*	1520	48.5%	

May 1955				*Con gain from Lab*
2. Edgar Anderson	*Con*	1750	58.8%	*Con maj 523 (17.6%)*
Violet Taylor	*Lab*	1227	41.2%	

May 1956				*Lab gain from Con*
3. Albert Kedge	*Lab*	1468	54.5%	*Lab maj 242 (9.0%)*
Harry Woolgar	*Con*	1226	45.5%	

May 1957				*No change*
1. Robert Davies (R)	*Lab*	1694	60.2%	*Lab maj 574 (20.4%)*
Dorothy Rowling	*Con*	1120	39.8%	

May 1958				*No change*
2. Edgar Anderson (R)	*Con*	1445	52.7%	*Con maj 147 (5.4%)*
John Clark	*Lab*	1298	47.3%	

East Chesterton (contd.)

May 1959				*Con gain from Lab*
3. Norman Tobin	*Con*	1431	50.9%	*Con maj 52 (1.9%)*
Albert Kedge (R)	*Lab*	1379	49.1%	

May 1960				*No change*
1. Robert Davies (R)	*Lab*	1402	52.5%	*Lab maj 132 (4.9%)*
Ernest Coe	*Con*	1270	47.5%	

May 1961				*No change*
2. Edgar Anderson (R)	*Con*	1257	56.3%	*Con maj 282 (12.6%)*
Josef Schicker	*Lab*	975	43.7%	

May 1962				*No change*
3. Norman Tobin (R)	*Con*	1313	51.9%	*Con maj 95 (3.8%)*
Matthew Winter	*Lab*	1218	48.1%	

May 1963				*No change*
1. Robert Davies (R)	*Lab*	1609	47.0%	*Lab maj 634 (18.5%)*
Anne Farmer	*Lib*	975	28.5%	
Sidney Hopkins	*Con*	836	24.4%	

May 1964				*Lab gain from Con*
2. Peter Eden	*Lab*	1488	54.8%	*Lab maj 259 (9.5%)*
Edgar Anderson (R)	*Con*	1229	45.2%	

June 1964 (byelection)				*No change*
1. Frank Ramsbottom	*Lab*	1140	52.3%	*Lab maj 101 (4.6%)*
Trevor Littlechild	*Con*	1039	47.7%	

May 1965 (2 vacancies)				*Con gain from Lab*
3. Trevor Littlechild	*Con*	1716	64.1%	
2. Arthur Howard	*Con*	1682	62.8%	*Con maj 691 (25.8%)*
Josephine Pryke	*Lab*	991	37.0%	
Joyce Matthews	*Lab*	967	36.1%	

May 1966				*Con gain from Lab*
1. William Crossman	*Con*	1581	55.9%	*Con maj 334 (11.8%)*
Frank Ramsbottom (R)	*Lab*	1247	44.1%	

May 1967				*No change*
2. Arthur Howard (R)	*Con*	1873	65.5%	*Con maj 886 (31.0%)*
Michael Deighton	*Lab*	987	34.5%	

East Chesterton (contd.)

Generaol re-warding: East Chesterton lost area from West Chesterton.

May 1968   *No change*
3. Stanley Granfield   *Con*   1423   69.5%   *Con maj 798 (39.0%)*
John Proud   *Lab*   625   30.5%

August 1968 (byelection)   *No change*
2. Walter Leach   Con   871   56.4%   *Con maj 198 (12.8%)*
John Proud   Lab   673   43.6%

May 1969   *No change*
1. William Crossman (R) *Con*   1401   71.7%   *Con maj 848 (43.4%)*
John Proud   *Lab*   553   28.3%

May 1970   *No change*
2. Walter Leach (R)   *Con*   1181   62.9%   *Con maj 485 (25.8%)*
Bridget Shaw   *Lab*   696   37.1%

September 1970 (byelection)   *No change*
1. Chris Gough-Goodman *Con*   796   49.8%   *Con maj 162 (10.1%)*
Bridget Shaw   *Lab*   634   39.6%
Bernard Greaves   *Lib*   170   10.6%

May 1971   *Lab gain from Con*
3. Julian Hunt   *Lab*   1226   52.1%   *Lab maj 99 (4.2%)*
Stanley Granfield (R)   *Con*   1127   47.9%

May 1972   *Lab gain from Con*
Michael Rooney   *Lab*   1189   51.6%   *Lab maj 75 (3.3%)*
Chris Gough-Goodman (R)   *Con*   1114   48.4%

June 1973 (All up elections - 3 vacancies, all retiring 1976)   *3 Lab*
Michael Rooney (R)   *Lab*   1158   57.5%
Leonard Freeman   *Lab*   1063   52.8%
Raith Overhill   *Lab*   1063   52.8%   *Lab maj 107 (5.3%)*
June Foote   *Con*   956   47.5%
David Bosley   *Con*   923   45.8%
Stanley Bowles   *Con*   881   43.7%   (R) Alderman

General re-warding: East Chesterton gained the area between Union Lane and Elizabeth Way.

East Chesterton (contd.)

May 1976 (All up elections - 3 vacancies)				*3 Con*
1. Graham Knowles	*Con*	1342	54.5%	
3. Sidney Reid	*Con*	1323	53.8%	
2. Sidney Miller	*Con*	1279	52.0%	*Con maj 315 (12.8%)*
Raith Overhill (R)	*Lab*	964	39.2%	
Leonard Freeman (R)	*Lab*	960	39.0%	
Anthony Carter	*Lab*	904	36.7%	(R) Cherry Hinton
May 1978				*No change*
2. Sidney Miller (R)	*Con*	1277	58.3%	*Con maj 365 (16.7%)*
Richard Wall	*Lab*	912	41.7%	
May 1979				*No change*
3. Sidney Reid (R)	*Con*	2057	47.2%	*Con maj 452 (10.4%)*
Richard Wall	*Lab*	1605	36.8%	
Anita Anderson	*Lib*	699	16.0%	
May 1980				*No change*
1. Graham Knowles (R)	*Con*	1245	45.7%	*Con maj 6 (0.2%)*
Carey Widdows	*Lab*	1239	45.5%	
Anita Anderson	*Lib*	238	8.7%	
May 1982				*No change*
2. Sidney Miller (R)	*Con*	1257	40.8%	*Con maj 305 (9.9%)*
Jonathan Hardy	*Lab*	952	30.9%	
Stephen Marshall	*SDP*	874	28.3%	
May 1983				*No change*
3. Sidney Reid (R)	*Con*	1320	41.0%	*Con maj 203 (6.3%)*
Peter Hall	*Lab*	1117	34.7%	
Christine Carling	*SDP*	786	24.4%	
May 1984				*No change*
1. Stephen George	*Con*	1355	43.4%	*Con maj 292 (9.3%)*
Vivien Allum	*Lab*	1063	34.0%	
Marion Simpson	*SDP*	705	22.6%	
May 1985 (byelection)				*Lab gain from Con*
2. Martin Blake	*Lab*	1199	35.1%	*Lab maj (22 0.6%)*
Peter Day	*Con*	1177	34.5%	
Simon Kightley	*SDP*	1037	30.4%	

May 1986				*Con gain from lab*
2. Peter Day	*Con*	1429	40.8%	*Con maj 182 (5.2%)*
Martin Blake (R)	*Lab*	1247	35.6%	
Victor Godfrey	*SDP*	824	23.5%	

May 1987				*No change*
3. Gordon Beckett	*Con*	1628	47.5%	*Con maj 615 (17.9%)*
Eleanor Fairclough (R)	*Lab*	1013	29.6%	(R) Abbey
Margaret Trowell	*SDP*	787	23.0%	

May 1988				*No change*
1. Stephen George (R)	*Con*	1460	48.6%	*Con maj 350 (11.6%)*
Mark Thompson	*Lab*	1110	36.9%	
Roman Znajek	*SLD*	437	14.5%	

May 1990				*Lab gain from Con*
2. Valerie Antopolski	*Lab*	1515	43.6%	*Lab maj 517 (14.9%)*
Geoffrey Howe	*Con*	998	28.7%	
Roman Znajek	*LDm*	776	22.3%	
Peter Pope	*Gre*	186	5.4%	

May 1991				*LDm gain from Con*
3. Roman Znajek	*LDm*	1083	33.7%	*LDm maj 50 (1.6%)*
Patrick Harding	*Con*	1033	32.1%	
Andrew Milbourn	*Lab*	1008	31.3%	
Peter Pope	*Gre*	94	2.9%	

May 1992				*LDm gain from Con*
1. Joseph Nunes	*LDm*	987	35.5%	*LDm maj 42 (1.5%)*
Alan Carter	*Con*	945	34.0%	
Michael Rooney	*Lab*	848	30.5%	

May 1994				*LDm gain from Lab*
2. Sheila Stickley	*LDm*	1402	46.0%	*LDm maj 206 (6.8%)*
Christopher Wilson	*Lab*	1196	39.2%	
Colin Havercroft	*Con*	453	14.8%	

May 1995				*No change*
3. Roman Znajek (R)	*LDm*	1412	47.2%	*LDm maj 168 (5.6%)*
Stephen Hartley	*Lab*	1244	41.6%	
Colin Havercroft	*Con*	333	11.1%	

East Chesterton (contd.)

May 1996				*No change*
1. Joseph Nunes (R)	*LDm*	1271	44.1%	*LDm maj 22 (0.8%)*
Stephen Hartley	*Lab*	1249	43.3%	
Colin Havercroft	*Con*	365	12.7%	

May 1998				*No change*
2. Fiona Levison	*LDm*	971	44.2%	*LDm maj 68 (3.1%)*
Tricia Charlesworth	*Lab*	903	41.1%	
Colin Havercroft	*Con*	324	14.7%	

May 1999				*Lab gain from LDm*
3. Patricia Johnston	*Lab*	1121	44.9%	*Lab maj 72 (2.9%)*
Jennifer Liddle	*LDm*	1049	42.0%	
Colin Havercroft	*Con*	325	13.0%	

May 2000				*No change*
1. Jennifer Liddle	*LDm*	1104	45.9%	*LDm maj 164 (6.8%)*
Sarah Woodall	*Lab*	940	39.1%	
Colin Havercroft	*Con*	361	15.0%	

May 2002				*No change*
2. Jennifer Bailey	*LDm*	974	40.5%	*LDm maj 116 (4.8%)*
Sarah Woodall	*Lab*	858	35.7%	
Mamunur Rashid	*Con*	319	13.3%	
Neil Hewett	*Gre*	129	5.4%	
Barry Hudson	*UKIP*	124	5.2%	

May 2003				*LDm gain from Lab*
3. Donald Adey	*LDm*	912	40.8%	*LDm maj 156 (7.0%)*
Patricia Johnston (R)	*Lab*	756	33.8%	
Mamunur Rashid	*Con*	332	14.8%	
Neil Hewett	*Gre*	157	7.0%	
Marjorie Barr	*UKIP*	79	3.5%	

General re-warding: East Chesterton lost the area north of Milton Road to King's Hedges.

East Chesterton (contd.)

June 2004				*3 LDm*
2. Jennifer Bailey (R)	*LDm*	913	40.7%	
1. Jennifer Liddle (R)	*LDm*	859	38.3%	
3. Donald Adey (R)	*LDm*	800	35.7%	*LDm maj 152 (6.8%)*
Pat Johnston	*Lab*	648	28.9%	
Geraldine Bird	*Lab*	616	27.5%	
Sarah Woodall	*Lab*	581	25.9%	
Marvin Goode	*Con*	392	17.5%	
Peter Pope	*Gre*	369	16.5%	
Louise Cadwallader	*Con*	363	16.2%	
Tina Goode	*Con*	334	14.9%	
Barry Hudson	*UKIP*	229	10.2%	

May 2006				*No change*
3. Marian Holness	*LDm*	884	40.6%	*LDm maj 301 (13.8%)*
Richard Layfield	*Lab*	583	26.8%	
Kevin Francis	*Con*	482	22.1%	
Peter Pope	*Gre*	228	10.5%	

May 2007				*No change*
1. Clare Blair	*LDm*	731	34.6%	*LDm maj 148 (7.0%)*
Kevin Francis	*Con*	583	27.6%	
Stefan Haselwimmer	*Lab*	457	21.6%	
Peter Pope	*Gre*	225	10.7%	
Peter Burkinshaw	*UKIP*	115	5.4%	

May 2008				*No change*
2. Jennifer Liddle	*LDm*	777	38.4%	*LDm maj 201 (9.9%)*
Kevin Francis	*Con*	576	28.5%	
Stefan Haselwimmer	*Lab*	368	18.2%	
Peter Pope	*Gre*	203	10.0%	
Peter Burkinshaw	*UKIP*	100	4.9%	

June 2009 (byelection)				*No change*
3. Susannah Kerr	*LDm*	836	37.6%	*LDm maj 284 (11.8%)*
Kevin Francis	*Con*	552	24.9%	
Samuel Wakeford	*Lab*	319	14.4%	
Peter Pope	*Gre*	313	14.1%	
Peter Burkinshaw	*UKIP*	201	8.8%	

East Chesterton (contd.)

May 2010 (2 vacancies)				*No change*
3. Susannah Kerr (R)	*LDm*	1477	36.6%	
2. Roman Znajek	*LDm*	1305	32.3%	*LDm maj 321 (7.9%)*
Kevin Francis	*Con*	984	24.4%	
Geraldine Bird	*Lab*	859	21.3%	
Una McCormack	*Con*	806	20.0%	
Dan Cooper	*Lab*	776	19.2%	
Peter Pope	*Gre*	634	15.7%	
Matt Ellis	*Gre*	581	14.4%	
Anna Gordon	*Soc*	137	3.4%	

May 2011				*Lab gain from LDm*
1. Geraldine Bird	*Lab*	1133	38.4%	*Lab maj 221 (7.5%)*
Clare Blair R	*LDm*	912	30.9%	
Kevin Francis	*Con*	488	16.5%	
Peter Pope	*Gre*	312	10.6%	
Peter Burkinshaw	*UKIP*	106	3.6%	

May 2012				*Lab gain from LDm*
2. Margery Abbott	*Lab*	1012	47.4%	*Lab maj 574 (26.9%)*
Tony Morris	*LDm*	438	20.5%	
Kevin Francis	*Con*	317	14.8%	
Peter Pope	*Gre*	241	11.3%	
Peter Burkinshaw	*UKIP*	129	6.0%	

May 2014				*Lab gain from LDm*
3. Peter Sarris	*Lab*	1076	35.5%	*Lab maj 10 (0.3%)*
Zoe O'Connell	*LDm*	1066	35.2%	
Peter Burkinshaw	*UKIP*	328	10.8%	
Peter Pope	*Gre*	299	9.9%	
Daniel John	*Con*	260	8.6%	

May 2015				*No change*
1. Geraldine Bird (R)	*Lab*	1630	38.8%	*Lab maj 465 (11.1%)*
Shahida Rahman	*LDm*	1165	27.8%	
J.Alexander Boyd	*Con*	608	14.5%	
Peter Pope	*Gre*	466	11.1%	
Peter Burkinshaw	*UKIP*	327	7.8%	

East Chesterton (contd.)

May 2016   *No change*

2. Margery Abbott (R)	*Lab*	1103	41.6%	*Lab maj 197 (7.4%)*
Shahida Rahman	*LDm*	906	34.2%	
Kevin Francis	*Con*	262	9.9%	
Peter Burkinshaw	*UKIP*	202	7.6%	
Jiameng Gao	*Gre*	179	6.7%	

May 2018 (2 vacancies)   *No change*

3. Carla McQueen	*Lab*	1362	50.5%	
2. Baiju Thittala	*Lab*	1107	41.1%	*Lab maj 277 (10.3%)*
Owen Dunn	*LDm*	830	30.8%	
Shahida Rahman	*LDm*	811	30.1%	
Gareth Bailey	*Gre*	345	12.8%	
Tom Harwood	*Con*	336	12.5%	
Timur Coskun	*Con*	299	11.1%	
Peter Burkinshaw	*UKIP*	93	3.5%	

May 2019   *No change*

1. Gerri Bird (R)	*Lab*	1097	44.1%	*Lab maj 270 (10.9%)*
Owen Dunn	*LDm*	827	33.2%	
Gareth Bailey	*Gre*	271	10.9%	
Timur Coskun	*Con*	165	6.6%	
Peter Burkinshaw	*UKIP*	128	5.1%	

No elections in 2020 due to Covid-19 pandemic

General re-warding (see map, near end of book)

May 2021 (All up elections – 3 vacancies)   *2 Lab 1 LDm*

1. Gerri Bird (R)	*Lab*	1463	49.2%	
2. Carla McQueen (R)	*Lab*	1023	34.4%	
3. Michael Bond	*LDm*	983	33.0%	*LDm maj 110 (3.7%)*
Baiju Thittala (R)	*Lab*	873	29.3%	
Bob Illingworth	*LDm*	773	26.0%	
John Leighton	*LDm*	696	23.4%	
Elizabeth May	*Gre*	623	20.9%	
Gareth Bailey	*Gre*	457	15.4%	
Peter Pope	*Gre*	430	14.5%	
Anette Iraninejad	*Con*	312	10.5%	
Frank Ribeiro	*Con*	272	9.1%	
Abubakar Said	*Con*	239	8.0%	
Peter Burkinshaw	*UKIP*	55	1.8%	

East Chesterton (contd.)

May 2022   *Lab gain*

3. Baiju Thittala	*Lab*	974	38.2%	*Lab maj 27 (1.1%)*
Bob Illingworth	*LDm*	947	37.1%	
Elizabeth May	*Gre*	388	15.2%	
Frank Ribeiro	*Con*	243	9.5%	

May 2023   *No change*

2. Alice Gilderdale (R)	*Lab*	1014	38.4%	*Lab maj 127 (4.8%)*
Bob Illingworth	*LDm*	887	33.6%	
Frank Ribeiro	*Con*	341	12.9%	
Elizabeth May	*Gre*	305	11.6%	
Colin Miller	*Her*	59	2.2%	
Peter Burkinshaw	*UKIP*	33	1.3%	

May 2024   *No change*

1.Gerri Bird (R)	*Lab*	1006	42.1%	*Lab maj 241 (10.1%)*
Bob Illingworth	*LDm*	765	32.0%	
Elizabeth May	*Gre*	368	15.4%	
Francisco Ribeiro	*Con*	251	10.5%	

May 2025 (byelection)   *LDem gain*

2.Bob Illingworth	*LDm*	871	33.1%	*LDem maj 115 (4.4%)*
Sarah Haithcock	*Lab*	756	28.7%	
Sarah Nicmanis	*Gre*	478	18.2%	
Mike Nicholson	*Rfm*	224	11.4%	
Steven George	*Con*	224	8.5%	

May 2026   *No change*

Sarah Haithcock	*Lab*	935	31.8%	*Lab maj 132 (4.5%)*
Ania Bobrowska	*LDm*	803	27.3%	
Isaac Groves	*Gre*	718	24.4%	
Godfrey Orr	*Rfm*	297	10.1%	
Jean-Ann Bartlett	*Con*	166	5.7%	
William Dry	*CPB*	18	0.6%	

~~~ King's Hedges ~~~

King's Hedges ward was formed in 1976, mostly from Arbury.

May 1976 (All up elections – 3 vacancies)				3 Lab
1. Peter Cowell ®	Lab	772	55.0%	® Arbury
3. Clarissa Kaldor	Lab	688	49.0%	® Arbury
2. Philip Geoghan	Lab	627	44.7%	Lab maj 47 (3.3%) ®*
David Parmenter	Con	580	41.3%	

(*Philip Geoghan ® Romsey)

May 1978				No change
2. Philip Geoghan ®	Lab	793	56.2%	Lab maj 319 (22.6%)
Malcolm Mackenzie	Con	474	33.6%	
Brian Badcock	Lib	145	10.3%	

May 1979				No change
3. Clarissa Kaldor ®	Lab	1544	52.3%	Lab maj 600 (20.3%)
Jacqueline George	Con	944	32.0%	
Brian Badcock	Lib	462	15.7%	

May 1980				No change
1. Peter Cowell ®	Lab	1134	70.6%	Lab maj 790 (49.2%)
Jane Jenkins	Con	344	21.4%	
Brian Badcock	Lib	128	8.0%	

May 1982				No change
2. Raith Overhill	Lab	811	48.0%	Lab maj 437 (25.8%)
Tristram Riley-Smith	Lib	374	22.1%	
William Sale	Con	358	21.2%	
Philip Geoghan ®	Ind	148	8.8%	See 1978

May 1983				No change
3. Andrew Burn	Lab	1117	49.5%	Lab maj 499 (22.1%)
Richard Smee	Lib	618	27.4%	
Andrew Dean	Con	523	23.2%	

May 1984				No change
1. Peter Cowell ®	Lab	1188	55.9%	Lab maj 589 (27.7%)
Richard Smee	Lib	599	28.2%	
Claire Barker	Con	340	16.0%	

King's Hedges (contd.)

May 1986   *No change*

3. Raith Overhill ®	*Lab*	881	52.2%	*Lab maj 463 (27.4%)*
David Howarth	*Lib*	418	24.7%	
Steuart Northfield	*Con*	370	21.9%	
Glenn Richer	*Comm*	20	1.2%	

May 1987 (2 vacancies)   *No change*

3. Stephen Hopkins	*Lab*	809	41.8%	
2. Jill Patterson	*Lab*	756	39.0%	*Lab maj 181 (9.3%)*
David Creek	*SDP*	575	29.7%	
Aidan Dodson	*Con*	507	26.2%	
Peter Hoskins	*Con*	500	25.8%	
Peter Warner	*SDP*	472	24.4%	

May 1988   *No change*

1. Peter Cowell ®	*Lab*	1175	65.2%	*Lab maj 780 (43.3%)*
Marilyn Hulyer	*Con*	395	21.9%	
David Creek	*SLD*	231	12.8%	

May 1990   *No change*

2. Jill Patterson ®	*Lab*	1307	61.5%	*Lab maj 926 (43.6%)*
Martin Graham	*Con*	381	17.9%	
David Creek	*LDm*	292	13.7%	
James Entwistle	*Gre*	144	6.8%	

May 1991   *No change*

3. Kevin Southernwood	*Lab*	999	57.3%	*Lab maj 534 (30.6%)*
Geoffrey Howe	*Con*	465	26.7%	
Stephen Warde	*LDm*	279	16.0%	

May 1992 (2 vacancies)   *No change*

1. Peter Cowell ®	*Lab*	871	58.4%	
2. Kevin Price	*Lab*	657	44.0%	*Lab maj 231 (15.5%)*
Geoffrey Howe	*Con*	426	28.6%	
Richard Baty	*Con*	390	26.1%	
Stephen Howarth	*LDm*	199	13.3%	
Stephen Warde	*LDm*	144	9.7%	

May 1994   *No change*

2. Angela Ratcliffe	*Lab*	1000	64.8%	*Lab maj 686 (44.5%)*
Edna Howarth	*LDm*	314	20.3%	
Sally Black	*Con*	229	14.8%	

King's Hedges (contd.)

May 1995				*No change*
3. Kevin Southernwood ®	*Lab*	1100	77.2%	*Lab maj 882 (61.9%)*
Evelyn Corder	*LDm*	218	15.3%	
Stephen Ryder	*Ind*	107	7.5%	

May 1996				*No change*
1. Peter Cowell ®	*Lab*	1116	77.0%	*Lab maj 919 (63.4%)*
Stephen George	*Con*	197	13.6%	
Rhodri James	*LDm*	136	9.4%	

May 1998				*No change*
2. Michael Talbot	*Lab*	613	65.1%	*Lab maj 436 (46.3%)*
Christopher Howell	*Con*	177	18.8%	
Tim Wesson	*LDm*	151	16.0%	

May 1999				*No change*
3. Raith Overhill ®	*Lab*	641	65.9%	*Lab maj 470 (48.3%)* ®*
John M Phillips	*Con*	171	17.6%	
Philip Rodgers	*LDm*	161	16.5%	
(* Raith Overhill ® Coleridge)				

May 2000				*No change*
1. Peter Cowell ®	*Lab*	644	64.3%	*Lab maj 440 (44.0%)*
Jason Webb	*Con*	204	20.4%	
Philip Rodgers	*LDm*	153	15.3%	

May 2002				*No change*
2. Maria Bell	*Lab*	550	54.6%	*Lab maj 315 (31.3%)*
Cyril Weinman	*Con*	235	23.3%	
Evelyn Bradford	*LDm*	157	15.6%	
Gerhard Goldbeck-Wood	*Gre*	65	6.5%	

May 2003 (2 vacancies)				*No change*
3. P.Elizabeth Hughes	*Lab*	473	50.6%	
2. Louise Downham	*Lab*	438	46.8%	*Lab maj 224 (24.0%)*
Hugh Mennie	*Con*	214	22.9%	
Cyril Weinman	*Con*	202	21.6%	
Evelyn Bradford	*LDm*	182	19.5%	
Jonathan Monroe	*LDm*	129	13.8%	
Gerhard Goldbeck-Wood	*Gre*	95	10.2%	

General re-warding: King's Hedges gained the area north of Milton Road from East Chesterton and Arbury Court from Arbury.

June 2004

3 Lab

2. Louise Downham ®	*Lab*	558	32.7%	
1. P.Elizabeth Hughes ®	*Lab*	550	32.2%	
3. Maria Bell ®	*Lab*	524	30.7%	*Lab maj 50 (2.9%)*
Peter Langley	*Con*	474	27.7%	
Michael Pitt	*LDm*	449	26.3%	
Philip Rodgers	*LDm*	424	24.8%	
D.Neale Upstone	*LDm*	407	23.8%	
Hugh Mennie	*Con*	404	23.6%	
Cyril Weinman	*Con*	369	21.6%	
Gerhard Goldbeck-Wood	*Gre*	244	14.3%	
Geraldine Roper	*Gre*	244	14.3%	

May 2006

LDm gain from Lab

3. D.Neale Upstone	*LDm*	718	40.0%	*LDm maj 185 (10.3%)*
Geraldine Bird	*Lab*	533	29.7%	
Mark T. Taylor	*Con*	350	19.5%	
Gerhard Goldbeck-Wood	*Gre*	193	10.8%	

May 2007

LDm gain from Lab

1. Michael Pitt	*LDm*	679	35.9%	*LDm maj 18 (1.0%)*
Geraldine Bird	*Lab*	661	35.0%	
Michelle Tempest	*Con*	368	19.5%	
James Youd	*Gre*	181	9.6%	

May 2008

LDm gain from Lab

2. Neil McGovern	*LDm*	760	40.6%	*LDm maj 198 (10.6%)*
Geraldine Bird	*Lab*	562	30.1%	
Cyril Weinman	*Con*	419	22.4%	
James Youd	*Gre*	129	6.9%	

May 2010

No change

3. Simon Brierley	*LDm*	1236	36.3%	*LDm maj 250 (7.4%)*
P.Elizabeth Hughes	*Lab*	986	29.0%	
Matthew Adams	*Con*	813	23.9%	
Alexandra Collis	*Gre*	274	8.1%	
Martin Booth	*Soc*	92	2.3%	

<h1 align="center">King's Hedges (contd.)</h1>

May 2011				*Lab gain from LDm*
1. Kevin Price	*Lab*	904	40.0%	*Lab maj 175 (7.7%)*
Michael Pitt ®	*LDm*	729	32.3%	
Anette Karimi	*Con*	390	17.3%	
Ian Tyes	*Ind*	137	6.1%	
Martin Booth	*Soc*	99	4.4%	

May 2012				*Lab gain from LDm*
2. Nigel Gawthrope	*Lab*	827	48.4%	*Lab maj 251 (14.7%)*
Neil McGovern ®	*LDm*	576	33.7%	
Anette Karimi	*Con*	199	11.7%	
Ian Tyes	*Ind*	105	6.2%	

May 2014				*Lab gain from LDm*
3. Martin Smart	*Lab*	831	41.2%	*Lab maj 438 (21.7%)*
D.Neale Upstone	*LDm*	393	19.5%	
Ian Tyes	*Ind*	287	14.2%	
Anette Karimi	*Con*	266	13.2%	
Michael Potter	*Gre*	242	12.0%	

May 2015				*No change*
1. Kevin Price ® *Lab*		1367	39.0%	*Lab maj 641 (18.3%)*
Hugh Newsam	*LDm*	726	20.7%	
Anette Karimi	*Con*	552	15.7%	
Dave Corn	*UKIP*	419	12.0%	
Angela Ditchfield	*Gre*	355	10.1%	
Ian Tyes	*Ind*	87	2.5%	

May 2016				*No change*
2. Nigel Gawthrope ®	*Lab*	981	54.5%	*Lab maj 748 (41.5%)*
Hugh Newsam	*LDm*	233	33.7%	
Dave Corn	*UKIP*	223	12.4%	
Anette Karimi	*Con*	212	11.8%	
Angela Ditchfield	*Gre*	152	8.4%	

May 2018				*No change*
3. Martin Smart ®	*Lab*	924	41.0%	*Lab maj 527 (29.5%)*
Daniele Gibney	*LDm*	397	17.6%	
Anette Karimi	*Con*	302	13.4%	
Angela Ditchfield	*Gre*	165	7.3%	

King's Hedges (contd.)

May 2019 (2 vacancies)					*No change*
1. Alexandra Collis	*Lab*	851	48.1%		
2. Kevin Price ® *Lab*		751	42.5%	*Lab maj 296 (16.7%)*	
Luke Hallam	*LDm*	455	25.7%		
Ewan Redpath	*LDm*	380	21.5%		
Angela Ditchfield	*Gre*	352	19.9%		
Eric Barrett-Payton	*Con*	190	10.7%		
David Corn	*UKIP*	181	10.2%		
Benedict Smith	*Con*	164	9.3%		

No elections in 2020 due to Covid-19 pandemic

General re-warding (see map, near end of book)

May 2021 (All up elections – 3 vacancies)					*3 Lab*
1. Jenny Gawthrope Wood *Lab*		1013	45.9%		
2. Alex Collis ® *Lab*		966	43.7%		
3. Martin Smart ®	*Lab*	750	34.0%	*Lab maj 323 (14.6%)*	
Andy McKay	*LDm*	427	19.3%		
John Ionides	*Con*	401	18.2%		
Julia Tozer	*Gre*	369	16.7%		
Mark Slade	*Gre*	367	16.6%		
Jenny Ward	*Con*	352	15.9%		
Laurence Van Someren	*LDm*	347	15.7%		
Adrian Matthews	*Gre*	340	15.4%		
Joshan Parmar	*LDm*	335	15.2%		
Rosemary Ward	*Con*	329	14.9%		
Lionel Vida	*WPB*	56	2.5%		

May 2022					*No change*
3. Martin Smart ®	*Lab*	968	50.6%	*Lab maj 585 (30.6%)*	
Rory Clark	*LDm*	383	20.0%		
Dan Kittmer	*Gre*	314	16.4%		
Mohammed Uddin	*Con*	248	13.0%		

May 2023					*No change*
2. Alex Collis ® *Lab*		798	39.2%	*Lab maj 148 (7.3%)*	
Delowar Hossain	*Con*	650	31.9%		
Fionna Tod	*LDm*	305	15.0%		
Adrian Matthews	*Gre*	285	14.0%		

King's Hedges (contd.)

July 2023 (byelection)   *Con gain*
2. M. Delowar Hossain *Con*   622   34.9%   *Con maj 24 (1.3%)*
Zarina Anwar   *Lab*   598   33.6%
Jamie Dalzell   *LDm*   418   23.5%
Elizabeth May   *Gre*   142   8.0%

May 2024   *No change*
1.Jenny Gawthrope Wood (R)   *Lab*   974   45.1%   *Lab maj 237 (11.0%)*
Nasrul Islam   *Con*   737   34.1%
Robin Brabham   *Gre*   231   10.7%
Fionna Tod   *LDm*   217   10.1%

May 2026   *No change*
Martin Smart (R)   *Lab*   713   27.2%   *Lab maj 109 (4.2%)*
Daniel Quinn   *Gre*   604   23.1%
Mahmuj Ahmed   *Con*   493   18.8%
John McKay   *Rfm*   376   14.4%
David Creek   *LDm*   295   11.3%
Zarina Anwar   *Ind*   106   4.0%
Eleanor Cooke   *Ind*   33   1.3%

~~~ Market ~~~

November 1935 (All up elections - 3 vacancies)   *2 Con, Ind*
2. Alexander Spalding (R) *Con*   615   64.6%
1. William Bowen   *Con*   596   62.6%   (R) Fitzwilliam
3. Arthur Lofts   *Ind*   533   56.0%   *Ind maj 88 (9.2%)*
Harry Case   *Con*   445   46.7%   (R) Bridge

December 1935 (byelection)   *Ind gain from Con*
2. Edwin Jackson (R)   *Ind*   unopposed

November 1936   *No change*
3. Arthur Lofts (R)   *Ind*   unopposed

November 1937   *No change*
1. William Bowen (R)   Con   unopposed

November 1938   *Con gain from Ind*
2. John Pretty   Con   unopposed

No elections held during World War II.

November 1945 (2 vacancies)   *No change*
3. Arthur Lofts (R)   *Ind*   614   63.6%
2. Robert Hensher   *Con*   392   40.6%   *Con maj 50 (5.2%)*
Cyril Stockbridge   *Ind*   342   35.4%
Norman Higgins   *Ind*   309   32.0%
Robert Pearson   *Con*   273   28.3%

November 1946   *No change*
1. William Richmond   *Con*   unopposed

November 1947   *No change*
2. Robert Hensher (R)   *Con*   unopposed

November 1948 (byelection)   *No change*
1. Walter Stockbridge   *Con*   unopposed

May 1949   *No change*
3. Arthur Lofts (R)   *Ind*   755   59.4%   *Ind maj 240 (18.9%)*
Henry Peake   *Con*   515   40.6%

Market (contd.)

May 1950					*No change*
1. Walter Stockbridge (R) *Con*		unopposed			
October 1950 (byelection)					*Con gain from Ind*
3. Marcus Bradford	*Con*	unopposed			
May 1951					*No change*
2. Robert Hensher (R)	*Con*	unopposed			
May 1952					*No change*
3. Marcus Bradford (R) *Con*		unopposed			
May 1953					*No change*
1. Walter Stockbridge (R) *Con*		879	79.2%	*Con maj 648 (58.4%)*	
Irene Galey	*Lab*	231	20.8%		
May 1954					*I.C gain from Con*
2. Robert Hensher (R)	*I.C*	500	52.7%	*I.C maj 51 (5.4%)*	
Lady Gray	*Con*	449	47.3%		
May 1955					*No change*
3. Marcus Bradford (R) *Con*		unopposed			
May 1956					*No change*
1. Walter Stockbridge (R) Con		414	52.8%	*Con maj 154 (19.6%)*	
Irene Harper	*RPA*	260	33.2%		
Frederick Chandler	*Lab*	110	14.0%		
September 1956 (byelection)					*Con gain from I.C*
2. Gilbert Weatherhead	*Con*	258	61.6%	*Con maj 138 (32.9%)*	
Irene Harper	*RPA*	120	28.6%		
Frederick Chandler	*Lab*	41	9.8%		
May 1957					*No change*
2. Gilbert Weatherhead (R) *Con*		349	70.4%	*Con maj 202 (40.7%)*	
George Mackenzie	*RPA*	147	29.6%		
May 1958					*No change*
3. Marcus Bradford (R)	*Con*	unopposed			
May 1959					*No change*
1. Walter Stockbridge (R) *Con*		unopposed			

Market (contd.)

May 1960				*No change*
2. Gilbert Weatherhead (R) *Con*		unopposed		

May 1961				*No change*
3. Marcus Bradford (R) *Con*		unopposed		

May 1962				*Lib gain from Con*
1. Peter Calvert	*Lib*	341	39.5%	*Lib maj 32 (3.7%)*
David Reynolds	*Con*	309	35.8%	
George Scurfield	*Lab*	213	24.7%	

May 1963				*Lib gain from Con*
2. Alex Ellinger	*Lib*	284	38.6%	*Lib maj 17 (2.3%)*
Gilbert Weatherhead (R)	*Con*	267	36.3%	
Cecilia Scurfield	*Lab*	184	25.0%	

May 1964				*No change*
3. Marcus Bradford (R)	*Con*	360	52.6%	*Con maj 35 (5.1%)*
Molly Wisdom	*Lib*	325	47.4%	

November 1964 (byelection)				*Con gain from Lib*
1. Frederick Robinson	*Con*	313	60.3%	*Con maj 107 (20.6%)*
Molly Wisdom	*Lib*	206	39.7%	

May 1965				*No change*
1. Frederick Robinson (R) *Con*		unopposed		

April 1966 (byelection)				*No change*
1. John Cuningham	*Con*	252	54.8%	*Con maj 44 (9.6%)*
Donald Hudson	*Lib*	208	45.2%	

May 1966				*Con gain from Lib*
2. John Keatley	*Con*	305	47.0%	*Con maj 77 (11.9%)*
William Frend	*Lib*	228	35.1%	
Alice Roughton	*Ind*	116	17.9%	

May 1967				*No change*
3. Norman Tobin	*Con*	324	55.3%	*Con maj 62 (10.6%)*
William Frend	*Lib*	262	44.7%	

Market (contd.)

May 1968				*No change*
1. John Cuningham (R)	*Con*	900	63.0%	*Con maj 600 (42.0%)*
David Murray	*Lib*	300	21.0%	
Graham Nurse	*Lab*	228	16.0%	

General re-warding: Market took area from Abbey and the old St Matthew's.

May 1969				*No change*
2. John Chaplin	*Con*	839	64.9%	*Con maj 385 (29.8%)*
David Murray	*Lib*	454	35.1%	

May 1970				*Lib gain from Con*
3. David Murray	*Lib*	569	50.2%	*Lib maj 5 (0.4%)*
Norman Tobin (R)	*Con*	564	49.8%	

June 1970 (byelection)				*Lib gain from Con*
1. Christopher Bradford	*Lib*	657	56.3%	*Lib maj 147 (12.6%)*
Chris Gough-Goodman	*Con*	510	43.7%	

May 1971				*No change*
1. Christopher Bradford (R)	*Lib*	1462	46.7%	*Lib maj 626 (20.0%)*
Peter Lee	*Lab*	836	26.7%	
Howard Harrison	*Con*	834	26.6%	

May 1972				*Lab gain from Con*
2. Jonathan Kitchen	*Lab*	1323	40.1%	*Lab maj 237 7.2%*
Molly Wisdom	*Lib*	1086	32.9%	
David Skidmore	*Con*	892	27.0%	

June 1973 (All up elections - 4 vacancies, all retiring 1976)				*4 Lib*
Kathleen Kessick	*Lib*	1070	40.6%	
Colin Rosenstiel	*Lib*	1061	40.3%	
Sydney Foott	*Lib*	1043	39.6%	Ind from 1976
Lavena Hawes	*Lib*	1042	39.5%	*Lib maj 56 (2.1%)*
J.Joseph Lee	*Lab*	986	37.4%	
Judith Findlay	*Lab*	978	37.1%	
Alison Barnes	*Lab*	937	35.5%	
Martin Smith	*Lab*	882	33.5%	
James McCrystal	*Con*	675	25.6%	
Christopher Curry	*Con*	641	24.3%	
Maureen Leach	*Con*	620	23.5%	
Stephen Allcock	*Con*	609	23.1%	

Market (contd.)

General re-warding: Market lost colleges West of Trinity Street / Kings Parade and North of Silver Street.

May 1976 (All up elections - 3 vacancies)				*2 Lib, Con*
2. Colin Rosenstiel (R)	*Lib*	839	35.2%	
1. Lavena Hawes (R)	*Lib*	807	33.9%	
3. Graham Edwards	*Con*	790	33.2%	*Con maj 7 (0.3%)*
Michael O'Hannan	*Con*	783	32.9%	
Kenneth Price	*Con*	776	32.6%	
Bernard Greaves	*Lib*	764	32.1%	
David Bleiman	*Lab*	725	30.4%	
Sydney Foott (R)	*Ind*	520	21.8%	see 1973
Pippa Berry	*Comm*	306	12.8%	

May 1978				*Ind gain from Con*
3. Margaret Reiss	*Ind*	1778	71.2%	*Ind maj 1060 (42.5%)*
Graham Edwards (R)	*Con*	718	28.8%	

May 1979				*No change*
1. Lavena Hawes (R)	*Lib*	2295	55.8%	*Lib maj 1329 (32.3%)*
Michael O'Hannan	*Con*	966	23.5%	
Mike Gunn	*Lab*	853	20.7%	

May 1980				*No change*
2. Colin Rosenstiel (R)	*Lib*	1036	50.8%	*Lib maj 470 (23.1%)*
Michael O'Hannan	*Con*	566	27.8%	
Gwilym Colenso	*Lab*	436	21.4%	

May 1982				*Lib gain from Ind*
3. Joye Rosenstiel	*Lib*	1092	47.5%	*Lib maj 466 (20.3%)*
Michael O'Hannan	*Con*	626	27.2%	
Anthony Carter	*Lab*	580	25.2%	

May 1983				*No change*
1. Lavena Hawes (R)	*Lib*	1092	42.0%	*Lib maj 326 (12.5%)*
John Phillips	*Con*	766	29.5%	
Maureen Fallside	*Lab*	741	28.5%	

Market (contd.)

May 1984				*No change*
2. Colin Rosenstiel (R)	*Lib*	1257	49.5%	*Lib maj 562 (22.2%)*
Maureen Fallside	*Lab*	695	27.4%	
A.Richard Jones	*Con*	492	19.4%	
Timothy Astin	*Eco*	93	3.7%	

May 1986				*No change*
3. Joye Rosenstiel (R)	*Lib*	1036	42.6%	*Lib maj 271 (11.1%)*
Richard Leggatt	*Lab*	765	31.5%	
Aidan Dodson	*Con*	439	18.1%	
Julian Paren	*Gre*	191	7.9%	

May 1987				*No change*
1. Lavena Hawes (R)	*Lib*	1202	40.7%	*Lib maj 176 (6.0%)*
Richard Leggatt	*Lab*	1026	34.8%	
Mark Cathcart	*Con*	724	24.5%	

May 1988				*Lab gain from Lib*
2. Richard Leggatt	*Lab*	1061	38.4%	*Lab maj 29 (1.0%)*
Colin Rosenstiel (R)	*SLD*	1032	37.4%	
Michael O'Hannan	*Con*	506	18.3%	
Mark Tester	*Gre*	164	5.9%	

May 1990				*No change*
3. Joye Rosenstiel (R)	*LDm*	1285	41.1%	*LDm maj 101 (3.2%)*
Kevin Southernwood	*Lab*	1184	37.9%	
Mark Waldron	*Con*	361	11.5%	
Alfred Droy	*Gre*	297	9.5%	

May 1991				*No change*
1. Andrew Lake	*LDm*	1344	49.5%	*LDm maj 523 (19.3%)*
Kevin Blencowe	*Lab*	821	30.3%	
Martin Graham	*Con*	353	13.0%	
Timothy Cooper	*Gre*	196	7.2%	

May 1992				*LDm gain from Lab*
2. Colin Rosenstiel	*LDm*	1313	49.2%	*LDm maj 463 (17.3%)*
Richard Leggatt (R)	*Lab*	850	31.8%	
Richard Harwood	*Con*	398	14.9%	
Timothy Cooper	*Gre*	109	4.1%	

Market (contd.)

May 1994				*No change*
3. Joye Rosenstiel (R)	*LDm*	1502	61.0%	*LDm maj 826 (33.5%)*
David Blunt	*Lab*	676	27.4%	
James Strachan	*Con*	286	11.6%	

May 1995				*No change*
1. Andrew Lake (R)	*LDm*	1125	50.4%	*LDm maj 366 (16.4%)*
Carol Atack	*Lab*	759	34.0%	
James Strachan	*Con*	221	9.9%	
Lois Hickey	*Gre*	127	5.7%	

May 1996				*No change*
2. Colin Rosenstiel (R)	*LDm*	1196	55.9%	*LDm maj 477 (22.3%)*
Eleanor Flood	*Lab*	719	33.6%	
Alexandra Hardie	*Con*	223	10.4%	

May 1998				*No change*
3. Joye Rosenstiel (R)	*LDm*	837	60.5%	*LDm maj 549 (39.7%)*
Andrew Jones	*Lab*	288	20.8%	
Julie-Ann Ing	*Con*	154	11.1%	
Adam Swallow	*Gre*	105	7.6%	

May 1999				*No change*
1. Michael Dixon	*LDm*	818	54.0%	*LDm maj 480 (31.7%)*
Andrew Jones	*Lab*	338	22.3%	
Jason Webb	*Con*	198	13.1%	
Adam Swallow	*Gre*	162	10.7%	

May 2000				*No change*
2. Colin Rosenstiel (R)	*LDm*	835	54.6%	*LDm maj 537 (35.1%)*
Andrew Jones	*Lab*	298	19.5%	
John M Phillips	*Con*	234	15.3%	
Adam Swallow	*Gre*	162	10.6%	

May 2002				*No change*
3. Joye Rosenstiel (R)	*LDm*	879	57.0%	*LDm maj 640 (41.5%)*
Samuel Chamberlain	*Con*	239	15.5%	
Michael Sargeant	*Lab*	238	15.4%	
Martin Lucas-Smith	*Gre*	187	12.1%	

Market (contd.)

May 2003					*No change*
1. Michael Dixon (R)	*LDm*	817	56.7%	*LDm maj 577 (40.0%)*	
James Orpin	*Con*	240	16.7%		
Martin Lucas-Smith	*Gre*	213	14.8%		
Paul Sales	*Lab*	171	11.9%		

General re-warding: Market lost Lensfield Road to Trumpington.

June 2004 (All up election – 3 vacancies)					*3 LDm*
3. Joye Rosenstiel (R)	*LDm*	824	41.3%		
2. Michael Dixon (R)	*LDm*	813	40.7%		
1. Colin Rosenstiel (R)	*LDm*	791	39.6%	*LDm maj 424 (21.2%)*	
Timothy Haire	*Con*	367	18.4%		
John Ionides	*Con*	357	17.9%		
Martin Lucas-Smith	*Gre*	344	17.2%		
Alan Mendoza	*Con*	339	17.0%		
Daniel Scott	*Gre*	325	16.3%		
Adrian Brink	*Ind*	263	13.2%		
Michael Smith	*Gre*	245	12.3%		
John Burnett	*Ind*	232	11.6%		
Sylvia Lynn-Meaden	*Ind*	225	11.3%		
Elizabeth Walter	*Lab*	219	11.0%		
Damian Counsell	*Lab*	206	10.3%		
Donald McCallum	*Lab*	193	9.7%		

May 2006					*No change*
1. Colin Rosenstiel (R)	*LDm*	772	42.7%	*LDm maj 380 (21.0%)*	
Timothy Haire	*Con*	392	21.7%		
Martin Lucas-Smith	*Gre*	359	19.9%		
Maureen Donnelly	*Lab*	285	15.8%		

May 2007					*No change*
2. Michael Dixon (R)	*LDm*	679	42.4%	*LDm maj 335 (20.9%)*	
Gregory Patten	*Gre*	344	21.5%		
Timothy Haire	*Con*	341	21.3%		
Lucy Sheerman	*Lab*	237	14.8%		

May 2008					*No change*
3. Tim Bick	*LDm*	645	44.1%	*LDm maj 303 (20.7%)*	
Sheila Lawlor	*Con*	342	23.4%		
Nick Dale	*Lab*	255	17.4%		
Shayne Mitchell	*Gre*	222	15.2%		

Market (contd.)

May 2010				*No change*
1. Colin Rosenstiel (R)	*LDm*	1697	43.0%	*LDm maj 803 (20.4%)*
J.Alexander Boyd	*Con*	894	22.7%	
Jack Toye	*Gre*	783	19.8%	
Pamela Stacey	*Lab*	571	14.5%	

May 2011				*No change*
2. Andrea Reiner	*LDm*	754	28.0%	*LDm maj 89 (3.3%)*
Oliver Holbrook	*Lab*	665	24.7%	
Alexandra Collis	*Gre*	651	24.2%	
Jeremy Waller	*Con*	620	23.0%	

May 2012				*No change*
3. Tim Bick (R)	*LDm*	615	35.6%	*LDm maj 110 (6.4%).*
Noel Kavanagh	*Lab*	505	29.3%	
Brett Hughes	*Gre*	349	20.2%	
Edward Turnham	*Con*	257	14.9%	

May 2014				*Lab gain from LDm*
1. Dan Ratcliffe	*Lab*	903	32.2%	*Lab maj 182 (6.5%)*
Maximilian Fries	*Gre*	721	25.7%	
Colin Rosenstiel (R)	*LDm*	678	24.2%	
Alex Boyd	*Con*	500	17.8%	

May 2015				*Gre gain from LDm*
2. Oscar Gillespie	*Gre*	1147	27.7%	*Gre maj 7 (0.2%)*
Danielle Greene	*Lab*	1140	27.5%	
Dom Weldon	*LDm*	1134	27.3%	
Daniel Coughlan	*Con*	726	17.5%	

May 2016				*No change*
3. Tim Bick (R)	*LDm*	777	38.5%	*LDm maj 60 (3.0%)*
Danielle Greene	*Lab*	717	35.5%	
Stuart Tuckwood	*Gre*	401	19.9%	
Barney Baber	*Con*	125	6.2%	

May 2018				*LDm gain from Lab*
1. Anthony Martinelli	*LDm*	866	43.5%	*LDm maj 122 (6.1%)*
Dan Ratcliffe (R)	*Lab*	744	37.3%	
Jeremy Caddick	*Gre*	229	11.5%	
Henry Mitson	*Con*	153	7.7%	

Market (contd.)

May 2019				*LDm gain from Gre*
2. Katie Porrer	*LDm*	870	48.6%	*LDem maj 392 (21.9%)*
Steve King	*Lab*	478	26.7%	
Emma Garnett	*Gre*	329	18.4%	
William Phelps	*Con*	112	6.3%	

No elections in 2020 due to Covid-19 pandemic

General re-warding (see map, near end of book)

May 2021 (All up elections – 3 vacancies)				*2 LDm 1 Lab*
1. Tim Bick (R)	*LDm*	983	39.7%	
2. Alice Gilderdale	*Lab*	960	38.8%	
3. Katie Porrer (R)	*LDm*	868	35.1%	*LDm maj 117 (4.7%)*
Anthony Martinelli (R)	*LDm*	856	34.6%	
Graeme Hodgson	*Lab*	751	30.3%	
James Youd	*Lab*	688	27.8%	
Nicola Elliott	*Gre*	628	25.4%	
Emma Garnett	*Gre*	436	17.6%	
Isabelle Thomas	*Gre*	342	13.8%	
Tania Oram	*Con*	221	8.9%	
Phoebe Pickering	*Con*	218	8.8%	
James Appiah	*Con*	194	7.4%	

May 2022				*No change*
3. Katie Porrer (R)	*LDm*	904	43.4%	*LDm maj 224 (10.7%)*
Hollie Wright	*Lab*	680	32.6%	
Nicola Elliott	*Gre*	364	17.5%	
Sam Hunt	*Con*	137	6.6%	

May 2023				*LDm gain from Lab*
2. Anthony Martinelli	*LDm*	796	41.2%	*LDm maj 125 (6.5%)*
Rosy Greenlees	*Lab*	671	34.7%	
Krzysztof Strug	*Gre*	283	14.6%	
James Appiah	*Con*	184	9.5%	

May 2024				*No change*
1.Tim Bick (R)	*LDm*	777	40.9%	*LDm Maj 111 (5.8%)*
Rosy Greenlees	*Lab*	666	35.1%	
Krzysztof Strug	*Gre*	310	16.3%	
John Marenbon	*Con*	146	7.7%	

Market (contd.)

May 2026				*No change*
Katie Porrer (R)	*LDm*	854	43.2%	*LDm Maj 262 (13.3%)*
Alex Sefton-Tromans	*Gre*	592	30.0%	
Edwin Addo	*Lab*	303	15.3%	
Mark Wells	*Rfm*	127	6.4%	
Panda Xiong	*Con*	99	5.0%	

~~~ **Newnham** ~~~

November 1935 (All up elections - 3 vacancies)   *WCA,I.C,Con*

1. Mary Webber	*WCA*	640	47.5%	(R) Castle
3. Charles Wolf	*I.C*	611	65.4%	
2. Francis Priest	*Con*	572	42.5%	*Con maj 102 (7.6%)* (R)*
Jane Salter	*Lib*	470	34.9%	(R) Castle
Malcolm Goodall	*Con*	430	31.9%	
Arthur Ransom	*Con*	391	29.0%	(R) Bridge
Dermot Freyer	*Lab*	298	22.1%	(R) Romsey

(* Francis Priest (R) Cambridge Without)

November 1936   *No change*

2. Francis Priest (R)   *Con*   unopposed

November 1937   *No change*

3. Charles Wolf (R)   *I.C*   unopposed

November 1938   *No change*

1. Mary Webber (R)   *WCA*   unopposed

No elections held during World War II.

November 1945 (2 vacancies)   *No change*

2. Francis Priest (R)   *Ind*   unopposed

1. Lady Bragg (R)   *Ind*   unopposed   (R) Trumpington (co-opted)

November 1946   *No change*

3. William Gourlay	*Con*	829	54.4%	*Con maj 134 (8.8%)*
Helen Adrian	*Ind*	695	45.6%	

November 1947   *No change*

1. Lady Bragg (R)   *Ind*   unopposed

May 1949   *Con gain from Ind*

2. Ernest Cherry	*Con*	1154	60.7%	*Con maj 407 (21.4%)*
Mary Cattley	*Ind*	747	39.3%	

June 1949 (byelection)   *Con gain from Ind*

1. M.Enid Henn   *Con*   unopposed

May 1950   *No change*

3. William Gourlay (R)   *Con*   unopposed

Newnham (contd.)

May 1951				*No change*
1. M.Enid Henn (R)	*Con*	unopposed		

May 1952				*No change*
2. Ernest Cherry (R)	*Con*	unopposed		

May 1953				*No change*
3. William Gourlay (R)	*Con*	unopposed		

May 1954				*No change*
1. M.Enid Henn (R)	*Con*	unopposed		

May 1955				*No change*
2. Ernest Cherry (R)	*Con*	unopposed		

May 1956				*No change*
3. Helen Culverwell	*Con*	953	77.5%	*Con maj 677 (55.1%)*
Muriel Lloyd-Prichard	*Lab*	276	22.5%	

May 1957				*No change*
1. M.Enid Henn (R)	*Con*	unopposed		

May 1958				*No change*
2. Ernest Cherry (R)	*Con*	unopposed		

May 1959				*No change*
3. Helen Culverwell (R)	*Con*	unopposed		

May 1960				*No change*
1. M.Enid Henn (R)	*Con*	unopposed		

May 1961				*No change*
2. Ernest Cherry (R)	*Con*	870	61.5%	*Con maj 326 (23.1%)*
Clarissa Kaldor	*Lab*	544	38.5%	

May 1962				*No change*
3. Helen Culverwell (R)	*Con*	712	50.9%	*Con maj 349 (25.0%)*
Clarissa Kaldor	*Lab*	363	26.0%	
Stanley Parnham	*Lib*	323	23.1%	

Newnham (contd.)

May 1963 — *No change*
1. M.Enid Henn (R) — *Con* — 812 — 50.2% — *Con maj 370 (22.9%)*
Nora David — *Lab* — 442 — 27.4%
Antonia Knowlson — *Lib* — 362 — 22.4%

May 1964 — *No change*
2. Albert Wallman — *Con* — 722 — 48.2% — *Con maj 226 (15.1%)*
Antonia Knowlson — *Lib* — 496 — 33.1%
Francesca Ashburner — *Lab* — 280 — 18.7%

May 1965 — *No change*
3. Helen Culverwell (R) — *Con* — 791 — 81.3% — *Con maj 609 (62.6%)*
Premandra Addy — *Ind* — 182 — 18.7%

May 1966 — *No change*
1. M.Enid Henn (R) — *Con* — 704 — 56.3% — *Con maj 157 (12.5%)*
Anthony Rottenburg — *Lib* — 547 — 43.7%

May 1967 — *No change*
2. G.Richard Wright — *Con* — 870 — 56.2% — *Con maj 407 (26.3%)*
Gwyneth Lipstein — *Lab* — 463 — 29.9%
Anthony Rottenburg — *Lib* — 214 — 13.8%

July 1967 (byelection) — *No change*
1. John Byrom — *Con* — unopposed

General re-warding: Newnham gained area from Castle.

May 1968 — *No change*
3. Diana Ker — *Con* — 1114 — 65.5% — *Con maj 527 (31.0%)*
Horace Fuller — *I.C* — 587 — 34.5%

May 1969 — *No change*
1. John Byrom (R) — *Con* — unopposed

May 1970 — *No change*
2. Colin Kolbert — *Con* — 1242 — 70.4% — *Con maj 720 (40.8%)*
Moira Steel — *Lib* — 522 — 29.6%

Newnham (contd.)

May 1971 (2 vacancies)   *2 Lab gains from Con*

3. Gwyneth Lipstein	*Lab*	1937	56.8%
1. David Keate	*Lab*	1897	55.7%	*Lab maj 479 (14.1%)*
Michael Tillotson	*Con*	1418	41.6%
Graham Edwards	*Con*	1395	40.9%
Charles Ward	*Ind*	170	5.0%

May 1972   *Lab gain from Con*

1. David Keate (R)	*Lab*	1851	56.9%	*Lab maj 449 (13.8%)*
Roy Doig	*Con*	1402	43.1%

June 1973 (All up elections - 4 vacancies, all retiring 1976)   *4 Lab*

Gwyneth Lipstein (R)	*Lab*	1798	61.6%
Ruth Cohen	*Lab*	1726	59.2%
Robert Edwards	*Lab*	1660	56.9%
Elizabeth Gard	*Lab*	1651	56.6%	*Lab maj 406 (13.9%)*
Peter Chivers	*Con*	1245	42.7%
Peter Masters	*Con*	1233	42.3%
George Reid	*Con*	1211	41.5%
Ian Benson	*Con*	1145	39.2%

General re-warding: Newnham lost the area North of Madingley Road & Chesterton Road to Castle (some to West Chesterton) and gained colleges West of Trinity St. / Kings Parade & North of Silver St from Market.

May 1976 (All up elections -3 vacancies)   *3 Lab*

1. Gwyneth Lipstein (R)	*Lab*	1306	43.2%
3. Ruth Cohen (R)	*Lab*	1221	40.4%
2. Robert Edwards (R)	*Lab*	1218	40.3%	*Lab maj 46 (1.5%)*
Brian Cooper	*Con*	1172	38.8%
John Shaw	*Con*	1110	36.7%
Patricia Robinson	*Con*	1106	36.6%
Andrew Gore	*Lib*	598	19.8%
Julian Cummins	*Lib*	590	19.5%
David Grace	*Lib*	550	18.2%

Newnham (contd.)

May 1978				*No change*
2. O.M.Wendy Nicol	*Lab*	1501	49.1%	*Lab maj 514 (16.8%)*
Ella Craigie	*Con*	987	32.3%	
Anthony Waite	*Lib*	567	18.6%	

May 1979				*No change*
3. Ruth Cohen (R)	*Lab*	2273	47.2%	*Lab maj 997 (20.7%)*
Phyllis Osbourn	*Con*	1276	26.5%	
Vivienne Alford	*Lib*	1263	26.2%	

May 1980				*No change*
1. Gwyneth Lipstein (R)	*Lab*	1215	47.9%	*Lab maj 363 (14.3%)* SDP 1981
Stanley Craigie	*Con*	852	33.6%	
Shirley Fozzard	*Lib*	467	18.4%	

May 1982				*No change*
2. Violet Cane	*Lab*	1028	36.4%	*Lab maj 91 (3.2%)*
David Bard	*Con*	937	33.2%	
Terence Moore	*SDP*	857	30.4%	

May 1983				*No change*
3. Ruth Cohen (R)	*Lab*	1308	37.9%	*Lab maj 85 (2.5%)*
David Bard	*Con*	1223	35.4%	
Margaret Reiss	*SDP*	922	26.7%	

May 1984				*No change (see 1980)*
1. Gwyneth Lipstein (R)	*SDP*	1204	37.8%	*SDP maj 152 (4.8%)*
Jean Glasberg	*Lab*	1052	33.1%	
David Bard	*Con*	925	29.1%	

May 1986				*No change*
2. Violet Cane (R)	*Lab*	1057	32.5%	*Lab maj 4 (0.1%)*
Christine Bondi	*SDP*	1053	32.3%	
Edward Connolly	*Con*	878	27.0%	
Stephen Lloyd	*Gre*	269	8.3%	

May 1987				*SDP gain from Lab*
3. Elsa Meyland-Smith	*SDP*	1496	39.1%	*SDP maj 210 (5.5%)*
Jean Glasberg	*Lab*	1286	33.6%	
Edward Connolly	*Con*	1040	27.2%	

Newnham (contd.)

May 1988				*Lab gain from SDP*
1. Eleanor Fairclough	*Lab*	1152	33.9%	*Lab maj 91 (2.7%)*
Gwyneth Lipstein (R)	*SLD*	1061	31.3%	
Ann Knight	*Con*	934	27.5%	
Catherine Wolfe	*Gre*	248	7.3%	

May 1990				*No change*
2. Jean Glasberg	*Lab*	1676	46.5%	*Lab maj 795 (22.1%)*
Mark Bishop	*Con*	881	24.4%	
Nicholas Whyte	*LDm*	638	17.7%	
Joel Smith	*Gre*	409	11.3%	

May 1991				*Lab gain from SDP*
3. Daphne Roper	*Lab*	1010	33.2%	*Lab maj 114 (3.7%)*
Kenneth Wheatcroft	*Con*	896	29.5%	
Pamela Strachan	*LDm*	857	28.2%	
Margaret Wright	*Gre*	278	9.1%	

May 1992				*LDm gain from Lab*
1. Joyce Baird	*LDm*	1075	35.3%	*LDm maj 98 (3.2%)*
Eleanor Fairclough (R)	*Lab*	977	32.1%	
Kenneth Wheatcroft	*Con*	760	24.9%	
Margaret Wright	*Gre*	178	5.8%	
Neil Costello	*USp*	58	1.9%	

May 1994				*LDm from Lab*
2. Christopher Lakin	*LDm*	1477	46.7%	*LDm maj 187 (5.9%)*
Asha Patel	*Lab*	1290	40.8%	
Graham Stuart	*Con*	394	12.5%	

May 1995				*No change*
3. Daphne Roper (R)	*Lab*	1391	48.9%	*Lab maj 241 (8.5%)*
Malcolm Schofield	*LDm*	1150	40.5%	
Jason Webb	*Con*	301	10.6%	

May 1996				*Lab gain from LDm*
1. Gillian Richardson	*Lab*	1282	45.3%	*Lab maj 33 (1.2%)*
Joyce Baird (R)	*LDm*	1249	44.1%	
Caroline Turnbull	*Con*	301	10.6%	

Newnham (contd.)

May 1998				_No change_
2. Christopher Lakin (R) _LDm_		1041	59.2%	_LDm maj 568 (32.3%)_
Trevor Critchlow	_Lab_	473	26.9%	
James Strachan	_Con_	243	13.8%	

May 1999				_LDm gain from Lab_
3. Nichola Harrison	_LDm_	1109	54.9%	_LDm maj 475 (23.5%)_
Edward Addison	_Lab_	634	31.4%	
Ann Watkins	_Con_	278	13.8%	

May 2000				_LDm gain from Lab_
1. Malcolm Schofield	_LDm_	1016	53.1%	_LDm maj 476 (24.9%)_
Gillian Richardson (R)	_Lab_	540	28.2%	
Ann Watkins	_Con_	358	18.7%	

May 2002				_No change_
2. Sian Reid	_LDm_	1134	55.5%	_LDm maj 762 (37.3%)_
H.Patricia Wright	_Lab_	372	18.2%	
Richard Normington	_Con_	326	15.9%	
Tandy Harrison	_Gre_	190	9.3%	
Nigel Douglas	_Ind_	23	1.1%	

May 2003				_No change_
3. Julie Smith	_LDm_	987	54.3%	_LDm maj 653 (35.9%)_
Laurence Tailby	_Con_	334	18.4%	
Miriam Lynn	_Lab_	257	14.1%	
Anna Gomori-Woodcock	_Gre_	239	13.2%	

General re-warding: Newnham lost 6 colleges to Castle.

June 2004 (All up election – 3 vacancies)				_No change_
2. Sian Reid (R)	_LDm_	1018	51.0%	
1. Julie Smith (R)	_LDm_	931	46.6%	
3. Roderick Cantrill	_LDm_	904	45.2%	_LDm maj 475 (23.8%)_
Peter Harding-Rolls	_Con_	429	21.5%	
C.Gail Kenney	_Con_	411	20.6%	
Anna Gomori-Woodcock	_Gre_	400	20.0%	
Anna Hodge	_Con_	395	19.8%	
Rita Gaggs	_Lab_	317	15.9%	
Richard Layfield	_Lab_	288	14.4%	
William Quinn	_Gre_	282	14.1%	
Daniel Sternberg	_Lab_	279	14.0%	

Newnham (contd.)

May 2006 *No change*

3. Roderick Cantrill (R)	*LDm*	974	46.2%	*LDm maj 499 (23.7%)*
James Strachan	*Con*	475	22.6%	
Joseph Powell	*Lab*	336	16.0%	
Anna Gomori-Woodcock	*Gre*	321	15.2%	

May 2007 *No change*

1. Julie Smith (R)	*LDm*	842	44.9%	*LDm maj 353 (18.8%)*
James Strachan	*Con*	489	26.1%	
Aneaka Kellay	*Gre*	300	16.0%	
Louis Coiffait	*Lab*	246	13.1%	

May 2008 *No change*

2. Sian Reid (R)	*LDm*	870	50.1%	*LDm maj 443 (25.5%)*
James Strachan	*Con*	427	24.6%	
Jennifer Butler	*Gre*	238	13.7%	
William Redfern	*Lab*	200	11.5%	

May 2010 *No change*

3. Roderick Cantrill (R)	*LDm*	1862	44.9%	*LDm maj 868 (20.9%)*
Stephen Oliver	*Con*	994	24.0%	
Leonard Freeman	*Lab*	648	15.6%	
James Youd	*Gre*	642	15.5%	

May 2011 *No change*

1. Julie Smith (R)	*LDm*	990	35.2%	*LDm maj 234 (8.3%)*
Richard Johnson	*Lab*	756	26.9%	
Joanna Anscombe-Bell	*Con*	621	22.1%	
James Youd	*Gre*	443	15.8%	

May 2012 *No change*

2. Sian Reid (R)	*LDm*	917	44.5%	*LDm maj 276 (13.4%)*
Sarah Cain	*Lab*	641	31.1%	
Andre Beaumont	*Con*	263	12.8%	
Billy Aldridge	*Gre*	241	11.7%	

May 2014 *No change*

3. Roderick Cantrill (R)	*LDm*	1056	35.6%	*LDm maj 69 (2.3%)*
Sam Wolfe	*Lab*	987	33.3%	
Julia Harrison	*Gre*	526	17.7%	
Joanna Anscombe-Bell	*Con*	395	13.3%	

Newnham (contd.)

May 2015 — *No change*

1. **Markus Gehring**	*LDm*	1387	32.7%	*LDm maj 184 (4.3%)*
Ewan McGaughey	*Lab*	1203	28.4%	
Kate Honey	*Gre*	947	22.4%	
Sam Carr	*Con*	700	16.5%	

May 2016 — *No change*

2. **Lucy Nethsingha**	*LDm*	939	43.2%	*LDm maj 152 (7.0%)*
Ewan McGaughey	*Lab*	787	36.2%	
Julius Carrington	*Con*	234	10.8%	
Mark Slade	*Gre*	216	9.9%	

May 2018 — *No change*

3. **Roderick Cantrill** (R)	*LDm*	1139	49.7%	*LDm maj 314 (13.7%)*
Mike Davey	*Lab*	825	36.0%	
Connor MacDonald	*Con*	165	7.2%	
Mark Slade	*Gre*	164	7.2%	

May 2019 — *No change*

1. **Markus Gehring** (R)	*LDm*	1003	50.1%	*LDm maj 451 (22.5%)*
Joe Besstall	*Lab*	552	27.6%	
Mark Slade	*Gre*	276	13.8%	
Dolly Theis	*Con*	171	8.5%	

August 2019 (byelection) — *No change*

2. **Josh Matthews**	*LDm*	774	59.5%	*LDm maj 539 (41.4%)*
Niamh Sweeney	*Lab*	235	18.1%	
Mark Slade	*Gre*	149	11.5%	
Michael Spencer	*Con*	143	11.0%	

No elections in 2020 due to Covid-19 pandemic

General re-warding (see map, near end of book)

Newnham (contd.)

May 2021 (All up elections – 3 vacancies)				*2 LDm 1 Lab*
1. Lucy Nethsingha	*LDm*	939	39.0%	
2. Niamh Sweeney	*Lab*	910	37.8%	
3. Markus Gehring (R)	*LDm*	844	35.0%	*LDm Maj 27 (1.1%)*
Cameron Holloway	*Lab*	817	33.9%	
Josh Matthews (R)	*LDm*	776	32.2%	
Hollie Wright	*Lab*	726	30.1%	
Beverley Carpenter	*Gre*	609	25.3%	
Shanna Hart	*Gre*	475	19.7%	
Brett Hughes	*Gre*	365	15.2%	
Wendy Fray	*Con*	196	8.1%	
James Vitali	*Con*	181	7.5%	
Mo Pantall	*Con*	148	6.1%	
May 2022				*Lab gain*
3. Cameron Holloway	*Lab*	813	36.4%	*Lab maj 75 (3.4%)*
Alastair Gadney	*LDm*	738	33.0%	
Jean Glasberg	*Gre*	558	25.0%	
Maureen Pantall	*Con*	125	5.6%	
May 2023				*Gre gain*
2. Jean Glasberg	*Gre*	895	40.5%	*Gre maj 139 (6.3%)*
Anne Miller	*Lab*	756	34.2%	
Chang Liu	*LDm*	398	18.0%	
Susie Williams	*Con*	161	7.3%	
May 2024				*Gre gain*
1.Hugh Clough	Gre	925	45.8%	*Gre maj 376 (18.6%)*
Yvonne Nobis	Lab	549	27.2%	
Lucy Nethsingha (R)	LDm	306	15.2%	
David Carmona	Ind	155	7.7%	
Susie Williams	Con	84	4.2%	
May 2026				*Gre gain*
Eleanor Toye-Scott	Gre	1046	53.0%	*Gre maj 719 (36.4%)*
Katie Barron	LDm	327	16.6%	
Sabina Harris-Hercules	Lab	308	15.6%	
Poppy Simister-Thomas	Con	162	8.2%	
Lui Murton	Rfm	89	4.5%	
David Carmona	Ind	42	2.1%	

~~~ **Petersfield** ~~~

November 1935   (All up elections - 3 vacancies)   *Ind, 2 Con*
1. Edward Church   *Ind*   843   44.1%   (R) South Chesterton
3. Justin Kenney (R)   *Con*   792   41.5%
2. Archibald Taylor (R)   *Con*   781   40.9%   *Con maj 19 (1.0%)*
Herbert Robinson (R)   *I.C*   762   39.9%
William James   *Con*   608   31.8%
Edward Smith   *Lab*   500   26.2%
Antoinette Price   *Lab*   499   26.1%

November 1936   *No change*
2. Archibald Taylor (R)   *Con*   921   68.3%   *Con maj 493 (36.5%)*
Antoinette Price   *Lab*   428   31.7%

November 1937   *No change*
3. Justin Kenney (R)   *Con*   unopposed

May 1938 (byelection)   *No change*
3. William James   *Con*   661   51.7%   *Con maj 43 (3.4%)*
Alec Clark   *Lab*   618   48.3%

November 1938   *No change*
1. Edward Church (R)   *Ind*   unopposed

No elections held during World War II.

November 1945   *No change*
2. Archibald Taylor(R)   *Con*   1003   50.5%   *Con maj 18 (0.9%)*
David Clarke   *Lab*   985   49.5%

November 1946 (2 vacancies)   *No change*
3. William James (R)   *Con*   1329   66.1%
1. Stewart Bull   *Ind*   1033   51.4%   *Ind maj 190 (9.5%)*
Grahame Shaw   *Lab*   843   42.0%
Walter Pitches   *Lab*   814   40.5%

November 1947   *No change*
1. Stewart Bull (R)   *I.C*   1681   68.1%   *I.C maj 895 (36.3%)*
Reginald Frost   *Lab*   786   31.9%

Petersfield (contd.)

May 1949				*No change*
2. Frank Pointer	*Con*	1642	68.7%	*Con maj 895 (37.5%)*
Harold Bowles	*Lab*	747	31.3%	

June 1949 (byelection)				*No change*
3. Sidney Pratt	*Con*	1163	67.1%	*Con maj 594 (34.3%)*
Harold Bowles	*Lab*	569	32.9%	

May 1950			*No change*
3. Sidney Pratt (R)	*Con*	unopposed	

October 1950 (byelection)				*No change*
2. Harry Davis	*Con*	1557	71.9%	*Con maj 948 (43.8%)*
Louis Dexter	*Lab*	609	28.1%	

May 1951			*No change*
1. Stewart Bull (R)	*Con*	unopposed	

May 1952				*No change*
2. Harry Davis (R)	*Con*	1516	59.6%	*Con maj 490 (19.3%)*
Ann Tweed	*Lab*	1026	40.4%	

May 1953 (2 vacancies)				*No change*
3. Leonard Cogman	*Con*	1323	65.2%	
1. John B Collins	*Con*	1292	63.7%	*Con maj 558 (27.5%)*
Wright Clayton	*Lab*	734	36.2%	
Florence Roden	*Lab*	708	34.9%	

May 1954			*No change*
1. John B Collins (R)	*Con*	unopposed	

May 1955			*No change*
2. Harry Davis (R)	*Con*	unopposed	

May 1956				*No change*
3. Leonard Cogman (R)	*Con*	660	41.0%	*Con maj 160 (10.0%)*
John Pettitt	*RPA*	500	31.1%	
William Smith	*Lab*	448	27.9%	

September 1956 (byelection)				*No change*
2. Arthur Arundale	*Con*	711	57.2%	*Con maj 178 (14.3%)*
William Smith	*Lab*	533	42.8%	

Petersfield (contd.)

May 1957				*No change*
1. John B Collins (R)	*Con*	645	50.9%	*Con maj 23 (1.8%)*
John Pettitt	*RPA*	622	49.1%	

May 1958				*No change*
2. Arthur Arundale (R)	*Con*	1004	54.9%	*Con maj 180 (9.8%)*
John N. Hughes	*Lab*	824	45.1%	

May 1959				*No change*
3. Leonard Cogman (R)	*Con*	900	66.1%	*Con maj 439 (32.3%)*
Lawrence Whittaker	*ILP*	461	33.9%	

May 1960				*No change*
1. John B Collins (R)	*Con*	763	54.7%	*Con maj 132 (9.5%)*
Lawrence Whittaker	*Lab*	631	45.3%	

May 1961				*No change*
2. Arthur Arundale (R)	*Con*	unopposed		

May 1962				*Lib gain from Con*
3. Bernard Keane	*Lib*	670	39.0%	*Lib maj 126 (7.3%)*
Paul Rayment	*Lab*	544	31.7%	
Leonard Cogman (R)	*Con*	503	29.3%	

May 1963				*Lab gain from Con*
1. George Scurfield	*Lab*	587	36.7%	*Lab maj 30 (1.9%)*
John B Collins (R)	*Con*	557	34.9%	
Stanley Parnham	*Lib*	454	28.4%	

May 1964				*Lab gain from Con*
2. Nora David	*Lab*	861	53.1%	*Lab maj 100 (6.2%)*
Arthur Arundale (R)	*Con*	761	46.9%	

May 1965				*Con gain from Lib*
3. Stanley Bowles	*Con*	842	49.4%	*Con maj 275 (16.1%)*
Yorick Wilkes	*Lab*	567	33.3%	
Dennis Chapman	*Lib*	294	17.3%	

May 1966				*Con gain from Lab*
1. Kenneth Carr	*Con*	780	46.4%	*Con maj 62 (3.7%)*
Rosemary Polack	*Lab*	718	42.7%	
Brian Matthews	*Lib*	184	10.9%	

Petersfield (contd.)

May 1967				Con gain from Lab
2. Robert Foote	Con	866	51.2%	Con maj 267 (15.8%)
Nora David (R)	Lab	599	35.4%	
Yvonne MacCallum	Lib	225	13.3%	

September 1967 (byelection)				No change
3. Veronica Chaytor	Con	675	47.1%	Con maj 120 (8.4%)
Nora David	Lab	555	38.8%	
Yvonne MacCallum	Lib	202	14.1%	

General re-warding: Petersfield takes area from old St Matthew's.

May 1968				No change
3. Veronica Chaytor (R)	Con	684	40.7%	Con maj 107 (6.4%)
Rev.Victor Dixon	Ind	577	34.3%	(R) St Matthew's
Josef Schicker	Lab	249	14.8%	
Yvonne MacCallum	Lib	171	10.2%	

May 1969				No change
1. Kenneth Carr (R)	Con	845	67.1%	Con maj 576 (45.8%)
Brian Shearey	Lab	269	21.4%	
Margaret Butcher	Lib	145	11.5%	

May 1970				No change
2. Robert Foote (R)	Con	899	61.2%	Con maj 330 (22.5%)
Roger Thornely	Lab	569	38.8%	

May 1971				Lab gain from Con
3. Roger Thornely	Lab	955	56.3%	Lab maj 213 (12.6%)
Veronica Chaytor (R)	Con	742	43.7%	

May 1972				Lab gain from Con
1. David Pearl	Lab	934	51.9%	Lab maj 280 (15.6%)
Brian George	Con	654	36.4%	
Phyllis Pink	Lib	211	11.7%	

June 1973 (All up elections – 2 vacancies, all retiring 1976)				2 Lab
Roger Thornely (R)	Lab	828	59.4%	
Rosalind Beveridge	Lab	811	58.2%	Lab maj 219 (15.7%)
Robert Foote (R)	Con	592	42.5%	
Peter John	Con	555	39.8%	

Petersfield (contd.)

General re-warding: Petersfield gained the area east of Sturton St, and the Riverside area, from Abbey.

May 1976 (All up elections - 3 vacancies)				*2 Con, Lab*
1. Elizabeth Sargent	*Con*	1018	44.3%	
3. Roger Thornely (R)	*Lab*	1013	44.1%	
2. Elaine Wheatley	*Con*	966	42.0%	*Con maj 5 (0.2%)*
David Mackie	*Lab*	961	41.8%	
Barry Wright	*Con*	948	41.3%	
Susan Trotman	*Lab*	936	40.7%	
Rosalind Beveridge (R)	*ILP*	460	20.0%	
May 1978				*Lab gain from Con*
2. Frank Gawthrop	*Lab*	1218	49.9%	*Lab maj 196 (8.0%)*
Elaine Wheatley (R)	*Con*	1022	41.9%	
L.Keith Edkins	*Lib*	201	8.2%	
May 1979				*No change*
3. Roger Thornely (R)	*Lab*	1899	48.9%	*Lab maj 527 (13.6%)*
Bridget Tasker	*Con*	1372	35.3%	
Joye Rosenstiel	*Lib*	613	15.8%	
May 1980				*Lab gain from Con*
1. E.Jill Tuffnell	*Lab*	1434	52.9%	*Lab maj 536 (19.8%)*
Elizabeth Sargent (R)	*Con*	898	33.1%	
Patrick Browne	*Lib*	236	8.7%	
Julian Paren	*Eco*	145	5.3%	
May 1982				*No change*
2. Frank Gawthrop (R)	*Lab*	1560	52.7%	*Lab maj 830 (28.0%)*
David Pearl	*SDP*	730	24.7%	
Matthew Butler	*Con*	671	22.7%	
May 1983				*No change*
3. Richard Robertson	*Lab*	1538	55.9%	*Lab maj 757 (27.5%)*
Geoffrey Clark	*Con*	781	28.4%	
Troy Cooper	*SDP*	431	15.7%	

Petersfield (contd.)

May 1984				*No change*
1. E.Jill Tuffnell (R)	*Lab*	1510	57.2%	*Lab maj 865 (32.7%)*
Steven Gardiner	*Con*	645	24.4%	
Andrew Lake	*SDP*	391	14.8%	
Guy Grimley	*Eco*	96	3.6%	

May 1986				*No change*
2. Frank Gawthrop (R)	*Lab*	1676	64.6%	*Lab maj 1113 (42.9%)*
Dianne Walton	*Con*	563	21.7%	
L.Keith Edkins	*Lib*	354	13.7%	

May 1987				*No change*
3. Richard Robertson (R)	*Lab*	1517	52.2%	*Lab maj 845 (29.1%)*
Steuart Northfield	*Con*	672	23.1%	
Andrew Lake	*SDP*	671	23.1%	
S.William Gill	*Ind*	44	1.5%	

May 1988				*No change*
1. E.Jill Tuffnell (R)	*Lab*	1679	66.3%	*Lab maj 1150 (45.4%)*
Christine Butler	*Con*	529	20.9%	
Andrew Paton	*SLD*	188	7.4%	
David Lenihan	*Gre*	138	5.4%	

May 1990				*No change*
2. Francesca Stevens	*Lab*	1751	60.9%	*Lab maj 1254 (43.6%)*
Audrey Hull	*Con*	497	17.3%	
Robert Graham	*Gre*	359	12.5%	
Andrew Paton	*LDm*	268	9.3%	

May 1991				*No change*
3. Beth Scott (Morgan)	*Lab*	1358	56.5%	*Lab maj 894 (37.2%)*
Peter Welton	*Con*	464	19.3%	
Andrew Paton	*LDm*	344	14.3%	
Guy Grimley	*Gre*	236	9.8%	

May 1992				*No change*
1. T.Benjamin Bradnack	*Lab*	1220	52.5%	*Lab maj 736 (31.6%)*
Dianne Walton	*Con*	484	20.8%	
Britt Meyland-Smith	*LDm*	456	19.6%	
Daryl Tayar	*Gre*	166	7.1%	

Petersfield (contd.)

May 1994   *No change*

2. Kevin Blencowe   *Lab*   1387   49.6%   *Lab maj 265 (9.5%)*

Catherine Bowden   *LDm*   1122   40.2%

Valerie Clayton   *Con*   285   10.2%

May 1995   *No change*

3. Colin Rogers   *Lab*   1259   48.9%   *Lab maj 344 (13.4%)*

Catherine Bowden   *LDm*   915   35.6%

Peter Welton   *Con*   249   9.7%

Margaret Wright   *Gre*   150   5.8%

May 1996   *No change*

1. T.Benjamin Bradnack (R) *Lab* 1456   62.4%   *Lab maj 871 (37.3%)*

Simon Goddard   *LDm*   585   25.1%

Peter Welton   *Con*   294   12.6%

December 1997 (byelection)   *No change*

3. Hannah Reed   *Lab*   664   58.5%   *Lab maj 478 (42.1%)*

Michael Dixon   *LDm*   186   16.4%

Peter Welton   *Con*   121   10.7%

Margaret Wright   *Gre*   117   10.3%

Laurence Jones   *Ind*   48   4.2%

May 1998   *No change*

2. Kevin Blencowe (R)   *Lab*   865   55.1%   *Lab maj 603 (38.4%)*

G.Stephen Smith   *LDm*   262   16.7%

Shayne Mitchell   *Gre*   248   15.8%

Peter Welton   *Con*   196   12.5%

May 1999   *No change*

3. Hannah Reed (R)   *Lab*   988   54.4%   *Lab maj 646 (35.6%)*

Shayne Mitchell   *Gre*   342   18.8%

Jason McCullagh   *LDm*   259   14.3%

Charles Harcourt   *Con*   227   12.5%

May 2000   *No change*

1. T.Benjamin Bradnack (R) *Lab* 896   49.7%   *Lab maj 505 (28.0%)*

Shayne Mitchell   *Gre*   391   21.7%

Kevin Wilkins   *LDm*   267   14.8%

Charles Harcourt   *Con*   249   13.8%

Petersfield (contd.)

May 2002   *No change*
2. Kevin Blencowe (R)   *Lab*   964   40.4%   *Lab maj 385 (16.1%)*
Kevin Wilkins   *LDm*   579   24.3%
Margaret Wright   *Gre*   514   21.5%
Lee Glendon   *Con*   257   10.8%
Jonathan Walker   *SoA*   72   3.0%

May 2003   *No change*
3. H.Patricia Wright   *Lab*   738   35.9%   *Lab maj 134 (6.5%)*
Kevin Wilkins   *LDm*   604   29.3%
Margaret Wright   *Gre*   481   23.4%
Daniel Whant   *Con*   235   11.4%

General re-warding: Petersfield lost the Riverside area to Abbey and areas south of
Fenner's and Station Road to Trumpington.

June 2004 (All up election – 3 vacancies)   *2 Lab, LDm*
2. T.Benjamin Bradnack (R) *Lab* 797   35.9%
1. Victoria Phillips   *LDm*   787   35.5%   became Victoria Bruce 2006
3. Kevin Blencowe (R)   *Lab*   770   34.7%   *Lab maj 43 (1.9%)*
Thomas Mortimer   *LDm*   727   32.8%
H.Patricia Wright (R)   *Lab*   709   32.0%
Jonathan Monroe   *LDm*   673   30.3%
John G Collins   *Gre*   349   15.7%
Ruhal Islam   *Gre*   345   15.5%
Shayne Mitchell   *Gre*   341   15.4%
Rosemary Clarkson   *Con*   273   12.3%
Donald Douglas   *Con*   230   10.4%
Laurence Tailby   *Con*   207   9.3%
Bernard Walker   *Ind*   89   4.0%

May 2006   *No change*
3. Kevin Blencowe (R)   *Lab*   879   39.0%   *Lab maj 31 (1.4%)*
Steven Cooper   *LDm*   848   37.7%
John G Collins   *Gre*   282   12.5%
Rosemary Clarkson   *Con*   243   10.8%

May 2007   *Lab gain from LDm*
1. Lucy Walker   *Lab*   1063   45.3%   *Lab maj 246 (10.5%)*
Steven Cooper   *LDm*   817   34.9%
James Martin   *Con*   239   10.2%
Shayne Mitchell   *Gre*   225   9.6%

Petersfield (contd.)

May 2008				*No change*
2. T.Benjamin Bradnack	*Lab*	857	44.3%	*Lab maj 316 (16.3%)*
Elizabeth Parkin	*LDm*	541	28.0%	
Jonathan Newton	*Con*	301	15.6%	
Simon Sedgwick-Jell	*Gre*	236	12.2%	

May 2010 (2 vacancies)				*LDm gain from Lab*
3. Sarah Brown	*LDm*	1571	40.9%	
2. Gail Marchant-Daisley	*Lab*	1237	32.2%	*Lab maj 237 (6.2%)*
Andrea Reiner	*LDm*	1000	26.0%	
Shayne Mitchell	*Gre*	923	24.0%	
Kevin Blencowe (R)	*Lab*	891	23.2%	
Hywel Sedgwick-Jell	*Gre*	575	15.0%	
Joshua Hordern	*Con*	558	14.5%	
Shapour Meftah	*Con*	472	12.3%	

May 2011				*No change*
1. Kevin Blencowe	*Lab*	1353	48.9%	*Lab maj 759 (27.4%)*
Zoe O'Connell	*LDm*	594	21.5%	
Shayne Mitchell	*Gre*	481	17.4%	
Shapour Meftah	*Con*	340	12.3%	

May 2012				*No change*
2. Gail Marchant-Daisley (R)	*Lab*	1036	56.6%	*Lab maj 714 (39.0%)*
Zoe O'Connell	*LDm*	322	17.6%	
Sandra Billington	*Gre*	263	14.4%	
Peter Patrick	*Con*	209	11.4%	

May 2014 (2 vacancies)				*Lab gain from LDm*
3. Ann Sinnott	*Lab*	1280	50.9%	
2. Richard Robertson	*Lab*	1223	48.6%	*Lab maj 503 (20.0%)*
Sarah Brown (R)	*LDm*	720	28.6%	
Matthew Hodgkinson	*Gre*	688	27.3%	
David Grace	*LDm*	317	12.6%	
Daniel Coughlan	*Con*	262	10.4%	
Linda Yeatman	*Con*	228	9.1%	

May 2015				*No change*
1. Kevin Blencowe (R)	*Lab*	1632	44.0%	*Lab maj 768 (20.7%)*
Atus Mariqueo-Russell	*Gre*	864	23.3%	
Elizabeth Parkin	*LDm*	795	21.4%	
Ben Flook	*Con*	422	11.4%	

Petersfield (contd.)

May 2016				*No change*
2. Richard Robertson (R) *Lab*		1305	61.4%	*Lab maj 984 (46.3%)*
Sharon Kaur	*Gre*	321	15.1%	
Daniel Levy	*LDm*	277	13.0%	
Catherine Durance	*Con*	221	10.4%	

May 2018				*No change*
3. Ann Sinnott (R)	*Lab*	1256	58.3%	*Lab maj 824 (38.2%)*
Sarah Brown	*LDm*	432	20.0%	
Virgil Ierubino	*Gre*	278	12.9%	
Simon Lee	*Con*	189	8.8%	

September 2018 (byelection)				*No change*
3. Kelley Green	*Lab*	873	47.9%	*Lab maj 210 (11.5%)*
Sarah Brown	*LDm*	663	36.4%	
Virgil Ierubino	*Gre*	171	9.4%	
Othman Cole	*Con*	115	6.3%	

May 2019				*No change*
1. Mike Davey	*Lab*	969	45.5%	*Lab maj 347 (16.3%)*
Sarah Brown	*LDm*	622	29.2%	
Virgil Ierubino	*Gre*	433	20.3%	
Stephen Burdett	*Con*	106	5.0%	

No elections in 2020 due to Covid-19 pandemic

General re-warding (see map, near end of book)

May 2021 (All up elections – 3 vacancies)				*3 Lab*
1. Mike Davey (R)	*Lab*	1590	48.0%	
2. Katie Thornburrow	*Lab*	1532	46.2%	(R) Trumpington
3. Richard Robertson (R)*Lab*		1362	41.1%	*Lab maj 447 (13.5%)*
Emmanuel Carraud	*LDm*	915	27.6%	
Judy Brunton	*LDm*	807	24.4%	
Jenny Richens	*Gre*	755	22.8%	
Cosmo Lupton	*LDm*	711	21.5%	
Edwin Wilkinson	*Gre*	540	16.3%	
Krzysztof Strug	*Gre*	472	14.2%	
Shapour Meftah	*Con*	346	10.4%	
David Thomas	*Con*	281	8.5%	
Robert Yeatman	*Con*	226	6.8%	

Petersfield (contd.)

May 2022   *No change*
3. Richard Robertson (R)*Lab*   1554   55.6%   *Lab maj 956 (34.2%)*
Emmanuel Carraud   *LDm*   598   21.4%
Edwin Wilkinson   *Gre*   456   16.3%
Mohammed Hossain   *Con*   188   6.7%

May 2023   *No change*
2. Katie Thornburrow(R) *Lab*   1302   49.5%   *Lab maj 793 (30.2%)*
Emmanuel Carraud   *LDm*   509   19.4%
Joshua Morris-Blake   *Gre*   449   17.1%
Paul Roper   *Con*   370   14.1%

May 2024   *No change*
1.Mike Davey (R)   Lab   1323   51.9%   *Lab maj 765 (30.0%)*
Zak Karimjee   Gre   558   21.9%
Sam Oliver   LDm   399   15.6%
Paul Roper   Con   226   8.9%
Christopher Wilkinson   FA   44   1.7%

May 2026   *Gre gain*
Kathryn Fisher   *Gre*   1363   40.9%   *Gre maj 155 (4.7%)*
Cameron Holloway (R Newnham)   *Lab*   1208   36.3%
Sam Oliver   *LDm*   412   12.4%
Luke Burrows   *Rfm*   182   5.5%
Paul Roper   *Con*   164   4.9%

~~~ **Queen Edith's** ~~~

May 1976 (All up elections - 3 vacancies)   *3 Com*

1. Elizabeth Hodder	*Con*	1677	58.1%	(R) Cherry Hinton
3. Sylvia Dolby	*Con*	1577	54.5%	
2. A.James Johnson	*Con*	1568	54.3%	*Con maj 948 (3)2.8%*
Peter Harper	*Lab*	620	21.5%	
George Rowling	*Lab*	619	21.4%	(R) Cherry Hinton
Ethel Shephard	*Lab*	615	21.3%	
M.Joan Fitch	*Lib*	597	20.7%	(R) Coleridge
U.Ann Corsellis	*Lib*	441	15.3%	
Stella Weeds	*Lib*	380	13.2%	

May 1978   *No change*

2. A.James Johnson (R)	*Con*	1569	70.3%	*Con maj 906 (40.5%)*
Stephen Dartford	*Lab*	663	29.7%	

July 1978 (byelection)   *No change*

1. Graham Edwards	*Con*	1371	60.2%	*Con maj 463 (20.3%)*
Stephen Dartford	*Lab*	908	39.8%	

May 1979   *No change*

3. Sylvia Dolby (R)	*Con*	2317	51.4%	*Con maj 1118 (24.8%)*
Ethel Shephard	*Lab*	1199	26.5%	
Alan Newman	*Lib*	990	22.0%	

May 1980   *No change*

1. Graham Edwards (R)	*Con*	1361	46.0%	*Con maj 345 (11.7%)*
Bruce Galloway	*Lib*	1016	34.4%	
Ethel Shephard	*Lab*	579	19.5%	

May 1982   *No change*

2. A.James Johnson (R)	*Con*	1486	44.9%	*Con maj 169 (5.1%)*
Lesbia Bradford	*Lib*	1317	39.8%	
Richard Robertson	*Lab*	507	15.3%	

May 1983   *No change*

3. Sylvia Dolby (R)	*Con*	1670	48.0%	*Con maj 386 (11.1%)*
Lesbia Bradford	*Lib*	1284	36.9%	
Patricia Winney	*Lab*	526	15.1%	

Queen Edith's (contd.)

May 1984				*No change*
1. Graham Edwards (R)	*Con*	1477	44.7%	*Con maj 239 (7.2%)*
H.Michael Allan	*Lib*	1238	37.5%	
Jan Burt	*Lab*	491	14.9%	
Corinne Garvie	*Eco*	97	2.9%	

May 1986				*No change*
2. Chris Gough-Goodman	*Con*	1456	44.1%	*Con maj 158 (4.8%)*
Lesley Bradford	*Lib*	1298	39.4%	
J.Emma Stiles	*Lab*	544	16.5%	

May 1987				*No change*
3. George Reid	*Con*	1622	45.5%	*Con maj 227 (6.4%)*
Patricia Reynolds	*SDP*	1395	39.2%	
Timothy Bedford	*Lab*	543	15.3%	

May 1988				*No change*
1. Graham Edwards (R)	*Con*	1550	48.9%	*Con maj 560 (17.7%)*
Alan Baker	*SLD*	990	31.2%	
Roger Fairclough	*Lab*	631	19.9%	

May 1990				*No change*
2. Chris Gough-Goodman (R)	*Con*	1319	40.0%	*Con maj 428 (13.0%)*
Andrew Hibbert	*Lab*	891	27.0%	
Lesley Bradford	*LDm*	886	26.9%	
Paul Martin	*Gre*	201	6.1%	

May 1991				*No change*
3. George Reid (R)	*Con*	1381	46.7%	*Con maj 514 (17.4%)*
Tricia Charlesworth	*LDm*	867	29.3%	
Janice Auton	*Lab*	711	24.0%	

May 1992				*No change*
1. Graham Edwards (R)	*Con*	1326	44.2%	*Con maj 244 (8.1%)*
Richard Darlington	*LDm*	1082	36.0%	
Pamela Henderson	*Lab*	595	19.8%	

May 1994				*LDm gain from Con*
2. Amanda Taylor	*LDm*	1703	51.1%	*LDm maj 790 (23.7%)*
Chris Gough-Goodman (R)	*Con*	913	27.4%	
Caroline Smith	*Lab*	717	21.5%	

Queen Edith's (contd.)

May 1995				*LDm gain from Con*
3. Anthony Mills	*LDm*	1388	47.3%	*LDm maj 617 (21.0%)*
John Beresford	*Lab*	771	26.3%	
Alexandra Hardie	*Con*	755	25.8%	
Luke Leighton	*NLP*	18	0.5%	

May 1996				*No change*
1. Graham Edwards (R)	*Con*	1138	37.7%	*Con maj 18 (0.5%)*
Ashley Woodford	*LDm*	1120	37.1%	
John Beresford	*Lab*	759	25.2%	

May 1998				*No change*
2. Amanda Taylor (R)	*LDm*	1394	54.8%	*LDm maj 592 (23.3%)*
Richard Williams	*Con*	802	31.5%	
Kira Davison	*Lab*	349	13.7%	

May 1999				*No change*
3. Ashley Woodford	*LDm*	1175	48.7%	*LDm maj 433 (18.0%)*
Richard Williams	*Con*	742	30.7%	
Kira Davison	*Lab*	371	15.4%	
Robert Milsom	*Gre*	126	5.2%	

May 2000				*LDm gain from Con*
1. Richard Stebbings	*LDm*	1282	54.9%	*LDm maj 571 (24.5%)*
Hilary Pennington	*Con*	711	30.5%	
Louise Downham	*Lab*	341	14.6%	

May 2002 (2 vacancies)				*No change*
2. Amanda Taylor (R)	*LDm*	1564	62.7%	*LDm maj 951 (38.1%)*
3. Alan Baker	*LDm*	1424	57.1%	
Keith Henry	*Con*	473	19.0%	
James Ray	*Con*	409	16.4%	
Frances Harper	*Lab*	342	13.7%	
Jean Stevens	*Lab*	258	10.3%	
Robert Milsom	*Gre*	160	6.4%	
Helene Davies	*UKIP*	78	3.1%	

Queen Edith's (contd.)

May 2003   *No change*

3. Alan Baker (R)	*LDm*	1497	63.8%	*LDm maj 1102 (47.0%)*
Keith Henry	*Con*	395	16.8%	
Susan Rosser	*Lab*	242	10.3%	
Robert Milsom	*Gre*	119	5.1%	
Helene Davies	*UKIP*	94	4.0%	

General re-warding: Queen Edith's gained the area between Hills Road and the railway from Trumpington and lost Cherry Hinton Road to Coleridge and Cherry Hinton.

June 2004 (All up election – 3 vacancies)   *3 LDm*

2. Amanda Taylor (R)	*LDm*	1671	59.9%	
1. Richard Stebbings (R)	*LDm*	1591	57.0%	
3. Alan Baker (R)	*LDm*	1566	56.1%	*LDm maj 913 (32.7%)*
Toby Edwards	*Con*	653	23.4%	
Mark Hall	*Con*	550	19.7%	
James Ray	*Con*	531	19.0%	
Brian Westcott	*Gre*	337	12.1%	
Leonard Freeman	*Lab*	277	9.9%	
Susan Rosser	*Lab*	256	9.2%	
John Kazer	*Lab*	211	7.6%	
Helene Davies	*UKIP*	206	7.4%	

May 2006   *No change*

3. Alan Baker (R)	*LDm*	1489	56.7%	*LDm maj 754 (28.7%)*
Donald Douglas	*Con*	735	28.0%	
Leonard Freeman	*Lab*	219	8.3%	
Shayne Mitchell	*Gre*	181	6.9%	

May 2007   *No change*

1. Viki Sanders	*LDm*	1364	53.4%	*LDm maj 604 (23.6%)*
Donald Douglas	*Con*	760	29.7%	
Leonard Freeman	*Lab*	221	8.6%	
Martin Lawson	*Gre*	210	8.2%	

May 2008   *No change*

2. Amanda Taylor (R)	*LDm*	1250	49.9%	*LDm maj 412 (16.5%)*
Donald Douglas	*Con*	838	33.5%	
Jonathan Goodacre	*Lab*	233	9.3%	
Martin Lawson	*Gre*	183	7.3%	

Queen Edith's (contd.)

May 2010 — *No change*

3. Jean Swanson	*LDm*	2129	49.0%	*LDm maj 908 (20.9%)*
Vincenzo Marino	*Con*	1221	28.1%	
Jonathan Goodacre	*Lab*	541	12.4%	
Brian Westcott	*Gre*	334	7.7%	
Carol Jackson	*UKIP*	122	2.8%	

May 2011 — *No change*

1. George Pippas	*LDm*	1318	41.1%	*LDm maj 488 (15.2%)*
Vincenzo Marino	*Con*	830	25.9%	
Sue Birtles	*Lab*	642	20.0%	
Brian Westcott	*Gre*	416	13.0%	

May 2012 — *Lab gain from LDm*

2. Sue Birtles	*Lab*	1084	39.7%	*Lab maj 121 (4.4%)*
Amanda Taylor (R)	*LDm*	963	35.2%	
Richard Jeffs	*Con*	513	18.8%	
Martin Lawson	*Gre*	172	6.3%	

May 2014 — *No change*

3. Timothy Moore	*LDm*	1362	42.6%	*LDm maj 411 (12.9%)*
John Beresford	*Lab*	951	29.7%	
Vince Marino	*Con*	522	16.3%	
Joel Chalfen	*Gre*	363	11.4%	

November 2014 (byelection) — *LDm gain from Lab*

2. Viki Sanders	*LDm*	933	36.5%	*LDm maj 143 (5.6%)*
Rahima Ahammed	*Lab*	790	30.9%	
Andrew Bower	*Con*	614	24.0%	
Joel Chalfen	*Gre*	222	8.7%	

May 2015 — *No change*

1. George Pippas (R)	*LDm*	1502	33.7%	*LDm maj 400 (9.0%)*
Matt Worth	*Lab*	1102	24.7%	
Andrew Bower	*Con*	1093	24.5%	
Joel Chalfen	*Gre*	546	12.3%	
Candido Channell	*UKIP*	213	4.8%	

Queen Edith's (contd.)

May 2016				*No change*
2. Jennifer Page-Croft	*LDm*	1189	43.0%	*LDm maj 388 (14.0%)*
John Beresford	*Lab*	801	29.0%	
Manas Deb	*Con*	544	19.7%	
Joel Chalfen	*Gre*	232	8.4%	

May 2018				*No change*
3. Colin McGerty	*LDm*	1259	44.2%	*LDm maj 432 (15.2%)*
Dan Greef	*Lab*	827	29.0%	
Manas Deb	*Con*	543	19.1%	
Joel Chalfen	*Gre*	218	7.7%	

May 2019				*No change*
1. George Pippas (R)	*LDm*	1067	36.8%	*LDm maj 229 (7.9%)*
Sam Davies	*Ind*	838	28.9%	
Dan Greef	*Lab*	464	16.0%	
Elizabeth Whitebread	*Gre*	329	11.3%	
Manas Deb	*Con*	205	7.1%	

No elections in 2020 due to Covid-19 pandemic

General re-warding (see map, near end of book)

May 2021 (All up elections – 3 vacancies)				*1 Ind 2 LDm*
1. Sam Davies	*Ind*	1874	56.0%	
2. Jenny Page-Croft (R)	*LDm*	1074	32.1%	
3. Daniel Lee	*LDm*	816	24.4%	*LDm maj 169 (5.1%)*
Richard Eccles	*LDm*	709	21.2%	
Indy Vadhia	*Lab*	647	19.3%	
Dan Zahedi	*Lab*	647	19.3%	
Conor Morrissey	*Lab*	554	16.6%	
Al Dixon	*Ind*	536	16.0%	
Christine Butler	*Con*	512	15.3%	
Jacqueline Whitmore	*Gre*	473	14.1%	
Peter Price	*Gre*	377	11.3%	
Simon Whitmore	*Gre*	318	9.5%	
Shoaib Shahid	*Con*	279	8.3%	
Suhaib Shahid	*Con*	199	5.9%	

Queen Edith's (contd.)

May 2022   *No change*
3. Daniel Lee (R)   LDm   1202   42.0%   *LDm maj 321 (11.2%)*
Steve King   Lab   881   30.8%
Jacqueline Whitmore   Gre   396   13.8%
Geoffrey Owen   Con   382   13.4%

May 2023   *No change*
2. Karen Young   *LDm*   1131   37.9%   *LDm maj 422 (14.1%)*
Thomas Ron   *Lab*   709   23.7%
Gordon Gregory   *Con*   580   19.4%
Jacqueline Whitmore   *Gre*   306   10.2%
Antony Carpen   *Ind*   261   8.7%

November 2023 (byelection)   *LDm gain from Ind*
1. Immy Blackburn-Horgan *LDm* 745   35.0%   *LDm maj 67 (3.1%).*
Thomas Ron   *Lab*   678   31.8%
David Carmona   *Con*   454   21.3%
Oliver Fisher   *Gre*   252   11.8%

May 2024   *No change*
1.Immy Blackburn-Horgan (R) *LDm* 1123   42.5%   *LDm maj 365 (13.8%)*
Bethany Gardiner-Smith   *Lab*   758   28.7%
Eric Barrett-Payton   *Con*   459   17.4%
Oliver Fisher   *Gre*   300   11.4%

May 2026   *No change*
Amanda Taylor   *LDm*   1503   49.0%   *LDm maj 947 (30.8%)*
Shayne Mitchell   *Gre*   556   18.1%
Maruf Ahmed   *Lab*   397   12.9%
Magnus Burt   *Con*   315   10.3%
Colin Bedson   *Rfm*   299   9.7%

<h1 align="center">~~~ Romsey ~~~</h1>

November 1935   (All up elections - 3 vacancies)   *3 Lab*
2. William Briggs (R)   *Lab*   unopposed   (R) alderman
1. William Few (R)   *Lab*   unopposed
3. Clara Rackham (R)   *Lab*   unopposed

December 1935 (byelection – 2 vacancies)   *No change*
2. Joseph Holt   *Lab*   1348   69.0%
3. Dermot Freyer   *Lab*   1323   67.7%   *Lab maj 717 (36.7%)*
John Read   *Con*   606   31.0%

November 1936   *No change*
3. Dermot Freyer (R)   *Lab*   unopposed

April 1937 (byelection)   *No change*
1. David Hardman   *Lab*   unopposed

November 1937   *No change*
1. David Hardman (R)   *Lab*   unopposed

November 1938   *No change*
2. Clara Rackham (R)   *Lab*   unopposed

December 1938 (byelection)   *No change*
3. Walter Paige (R)   *Lab*   unopposed

No elections held during World War II. George Proctor co-opted.

November 1945   *No change*
3. George Proctor (R)   *Lab*   unopposed

December 1945 (byelection)   *No change*
1. Thomas Amey   *Lab*   1817   67.8%   *Lab maj 953 (35.5%)*
Harold Ridgeon   *Con*   864   32.2%

November 1946   *No change*
2. Clara Rackham (R)   *Lab*   unopposed

November 1947   *No change*
3. George Proctor (R)   *Lab*   unopposed

Romsey (contd.)

May 1949   *No change*
1. Thomas Amey (R)   *Lab*   unopposed

May 1950   *No change*
2. A.Leslie Symonds   *Lab*   2218   66.6%   *Lab maj 1107 (33.3%)*
Leonard Cogman   *Con*   1111   33.4%

May 1951   *No change*
3. Harold Bowles   *Lab*   1500   54.8%   *Lab maj 262 (9.6%)*
Leonard Cogman   *Con*   1238   45.2%

May 1952   *No change*
1. Thomas Amey (R)   *Lab*   unopposed

May 1953   *No change*
2. A.Leslie Symonds (R)   *Lab*   unopposed

May 1954   *No change*
3. Harold Bowles (R)   *Lab*   1657   59.4%   *Lab maj 524 (18.8%)*
Walter Crysell   *Con*   1133   40.6%

May 1955   *No change*
1. Thomas Amey (R)   *Lab*   unopposed

May 1956   *No change*
2. A.Leslie Symonds (R)   *Lab*   1513   69.1%   *Lab maj 837 (38.2%)*
Donald Hudson   *RPA*   676   30.9%

June 1956 (byelection)   *No change*
1. Mervyn Stockwood   *Lab*   1050   64.7%   *Lab maj 476 (29.3%)*
Donald Hudson   *RPA*   574   35.3%

May 1957   *No change*
3. Muriel Lloyd-Prichard   *Lab*   1390   69.4%   *Lab maj 777 (38.8%)*
Donald Hudson   *RPA*   613   30.6%

May 1958   *No change*
1. Mervyn Stockwood (R) *Lab*   unopposed

June 1958 (byelection)   *No change*
2. Ernest Gill   *Lab*   unopposed

Romsey (contd.)

May 1959 (2 vacancies)				*No change*
2. Dorothy Howlett	*Lab*	unopposed		
1. Ernest Gill (R)	*Lab*	unopposed		Order determined by lot

November 1959 (byelection)				*No change*
3. Peter Wright	*Lab*	unopposed		

May 1960				*No change*
3. Peter Wright (R)	*Lab*	unopposed		

May 1961				*No change*
1. Ernest Gill (R)	*Lab*	unopposed		

May 1962				*No change*
2. Dorothy Howlett (R)	*Lab*	unopposed		

May 1963				*No change*
3. Peter Wright (R)	*Lab*	1608	56.2%	*Lab maj 356 (12.4%)*
Iain Fowler	*Lib*	1252	43.8%	

May 1964				*No change*
1. Ernest Gill (R)	*Lab*	1740	73.0%	*Lab maj 1097 (46.0%)*
Phyllis Pink	*Lib*	643	27.0%	

May 1965				*No change*
2. Dorothy Howlett (R)	*Lab*	1222	91.5%	*Lab maj 1109 (83.1%)*
Reuben Holland	*ILP*	113	8.5%	

September 1965 (byelection)				*No change*
1. Robert May	*Lab*	1148	61.6%	*Lab maj 431 (23.1%)*
Peter Knowlson	*Lib*	717	38.4%	

May 1966				*No change*
3. Peter Wright (R)	*Lab*	unopposed		

May 1967				*No change*
1. Robert May (R)	*Lab*	1055	67.6%	*Lab maj 549 (35.2%)*
Bernard Greaves	*Lib*	506	32.4%	

General re-warding: Romsey gained from Cherry Hinto

Romsey (contd.)

May 1968				*No change*
2. Nora David	*Lab*	984	49.1%	*Lab maj 120 (6.0%)*
Gerald Speed	*Con*	864	43.1%	
Bernard Greaves	*Y.L*	155	7.7%	

May 1969				*No change*
3. Peter Wright (R)	*Lab*	1247	59.4%	*Lab maj 396 (18.9%)*
Michael French	*Con*	851	40.6%	

May 1970			*No change*
1. Robert May (R)	*Lab*	unopposed	

May 1971				*No change*
2. Nora David (R)	*Lab*	1789	75.5%	*Lab maj 1208 (51.0%)*
Ralph Niblett	*Con*	581	24.5%	

May 1972			*No change*
3. Peter Wright (R)	*Lab*	unopposed	

June 1973 (All up elections – 3 vacancies, all retiring 1976)				*3 Lab*
Peter Wright (R)	*Lab*	1446	78.3%	
Robert May (R)	*Lab*	1293	70.0%	
Philip Geoghan	*Lab*	1273	68.9%	*Lab maj 753 (40.8%)*
Elaine Wheatley	*Con*	520	28.2%	
Alan Attesley	*Con*	510	27.6%	
Veronica Chaytor	*Con*	497	26.9%	

General re-warding: Romsey swapped areas south of Mill Road with Coleridge.

May 1976 (All up elections – 3 vacancies)				*3 Lab*
1. Peter Wright (R)	*Lab*	971	46.9%	
3. Robert May (R)	*Lab*	879	42.5%	
2. Terence Sweeney	*Lab*	860	41.6%	*Lab maj 153 (7.4%)* (R) *
Colin Barker	*Con*	707	34.2%	
Alan Charlesworth	*Lib*	469	22.7%	
John Steward	*Lib*	369	17.8%	
S.John Minton	*Lib*	356	17.2%	

(* Terence Sweeney (R) Cherry Hinton)

Romsey (contd.)

<table>
<tr><td>May 1978</td><td></td><td></td><td></td><td align="right">No change</td></tr>
<tr><td>2. Terence Sweeney (R)</td><td>Lab</td><td>989</td><td>49.4%</td><td>Lab maj 388 (19.4%)</td></tr>
<tr><td>Philip Robinson</td><td>Con</td><td>601</td><td>30.0%</td><td></td></tr>
<tr><td>Alan Charlesworth</td><td>Lib</td><td>380</td><td>19.0%</td><td></td></tr>
<tr><td>Julian Chaloner</td><td>Comm</td><td>31</td><td>1.5%</td><td></td></tr>
<tr><td colspan="5"> </td></tr>
<tr><td>May 1979</td><td></td><td></td><td></td><td align="right">No change</td></tr>
<tr><td>2. Robert May (R)</td><td>Lab</td><td>1891</td><td>49.3%</td><td>Lab maj 698 (18.2%)</td></tr>
<tr><td>Stephen Clarke</td><td>Con</td><td>1193</td><td>31.1%</td><td></td></tr>
<tr><td>Anthony Waite</td><td>Lib</td><td>748</td><td>19.5%</td><td></td></tr>
<tr><td colspan="5"> </td></tr>
<tr><td>May 1980</td><td></td><td></td><td></td><td align="right">No change</td></tr>
<tr><td>1. Peter Wright (R)</td><td>Lab</td><td>1214</td><td>59.3%</td><td>Lab maj 661 (32.3%)</td></tr>
<tr><td>Barry Wright</td><td>Con</td><td>553</td><td>27.0%</td><td></td></tr>
<tr><td>Richard Folley</td><td>Lib</td><td>279</td><td>13.6%</td><td></td></tr>
<tr><td colspan="5"> </td></tr>
<tr><td>December 1981 (byelection)</td><td></td><td></td><td></td><td align="right">SDP gain from Lab</td></tr>
<tr><td>3. Cathy Grove</td><td>SDP</td><td>947</td><td>47.6%</td><td>SDP maj 85 (4.3%)</td></tr>
<tr><td>Leonard Freeman</td><td>Lab</td><td>862</td><td>43.3%</td><td></td></tr>
<tr><td>Stephen George</td><td>Con</td><td>180</td><td>9.0%</td><td></td></tr>
<tr><td colspan="5"> </td></tr>
<tr><td>May 1982</td><td></td><td></td><td></td><td align="right">No change</td></tr>
<tr><td>2. Terence Sweeney (R)</td><td>Lab</td><td>1189</td><td>45.8%</td><td>Lab maj 182 (7.0%)</td></tr>
<tr><td>Richard Folley</td><td>Lib</td><td>1007</td><td>38.8%</td><td></td></tr>
<tr><td>Anthony Hay</td><td>Con</td><td>376</td><td>14.5%</td><td></td></tr>
<tr><td>Martin Booth</td><td>WRP</td><td>25</td><td>1.0%</td><td></td></tr>
<tr><td colspan="5"> </td></tr>
<tr><td>May 1983</td><td></td><td></td><td></td><td align="right">Lab gain from SDP</td></tr>
<tr><td>3. Simon Sedgwick-Jell</td><td>Lab</td><td>1263</td><td>40.3%</td><td>Lab maj 34 (1.1%)</td></tr>
<tr><td>Cathy Grove (R)</td><td>SDP</td><td>1229</td><td>39.2%</td><td></td></tr>
<tr><td>Julia Clark</td><td>Con</td><td>552</td><td>17.6%</td><td></td></tr>
<tr><td>Guy Grimley</td><td>Eco</td><td>90</td><td>2.9%</td><td></td></tr>
<tr><td colspan="5"> </td></tr>
<tr><td>May 1984</td><td></td><td></td><td></td><td align="right">No change</td></tr>
<tr><td>1. Peter Wright (R)</td><td>Lab</td><td>1497</td><td>55.0%</td><td>Lab maj 783 (28.8%)</td></tr>
<tr><td>Gale Waller</td><td>Lib</td><td>714</td><td>26.3%</td><td></td></tr>
<tr><td>Colin Barker</td><td>Con</td><td>509</td><td>18.7%</td><td></td></tr>
<tr><td colspan="5"> </td></tr>
<tr><td>May 1986</td><td></td><td></td><td></td><td align="right">No change</td></tr>
<tr><td>2. Terence Sweeney (R)</td><td>Lab</td><td>1261</td><td>58.5%</td><td>Lab maj 740 (34.3%)</td></tr>
<tr><td>Colin Barker</td><td>Con</td><td>521</td><td>24.2%</td><td></td></tr>
<tr><td>Carla Hurrell</td><td>SDP</td><td>373</td><td>17.3%</td><td></td></tr>
</table>

Romsey (contd.)

May 1987				*No change*
3. Simon Sedgwick-Jell (R) *Lab*		1304	50.5%	*Lab maj 549 (21.3%)*
Rosemary Wheeler	*Con*	755	29.3%	
Karen Anderson	*Lib*	522	20.2%	

May 1988				*No change*
1. Peter Wright (R)	*Lab*	1295	51.1%	*Lab maj 662 (26.1%)*
Lee Jones	*SLD*	633	25.0%	
Rosemary Wheeler	*Con*	492	19.4%	
David Fox	*Gre*	114	4.5%	

July 1988 (byelection)				*No change*
2. Barry Gardiner	*Lab*	1101	53.1%	*Lab maj 496 (23.9%)*
Lee Jones	*SLD*	605	29.2%	
Rosemary Wheeler	*Con*	367	17.7%	

May 1990				*No change*
2. Barry Gardiner (R)	*Lab*	1525	60.7%	*Lab maj 1158 (46.1%)*
Rosemary Wheeler	*Con*	367	14.6%	
Janice Corn	*LDm*	351	14.0%	
Ian Miller	*Gre*	271	10.8%	

May 1991				*No change*
3. Simon Sedgwick-Jell (R) *Lab*		1111	52.5%	*Lab maj 698 (33.0%)*
Thomas Timmons	*LDm*	413	19.5%	
Jason Webb	*Con*	376	17.8%	
Ian Miller	*Gre*	217	10.3%	

May 1992				*No change*
1. Peter Wright (R)	*Lab*	1002	55.8%	*Lab maj 622 (34.7%)*
Rachel Atherton	*Con*	380	21.2%	
Rupert Ford	*LDm*	262	14.6%	
Ian Miller	*Gre*	151	8.4%	

July 1993 (byelection)				*No change*
1. John Heywood	*Lab*	1038	45.6%	*Lab maj 52 (2.3%)*
Catherine Smart	*LDm*	986	43.3%	
Kenneth Sharpe	*Con*	166	7.3%	
Ian Miller	*Gre*	88	3.9%	

Romsey (contd.)

May 1994 — *No change*

2. John Ratcliff	*Lab*	1344	50.6%	*Lab maj 308 (11.6%)*
Catherine Smart	*LDm*	1036	39.0%	
Stephen Wren	*Con*	160	6.0%	
Ian Miller	*Gre*	118	4.4%	

May 1995 — *No change*

3. David Baxter	*Lab*	1238	53.2%	*Lab maj 409 (17.6%)*
Catherine Smart	*LDm*	829	35.6%	
Adam Cannon	*Con*	133	5.7%	
Ian Miller	*Gre*	114	4.9%	
M.L.Patrice Gladwin	*NLP*	15	0.6%	

May 1996 — *No change*

1. Adrian Lucas	*Lab*	1184	55.5%	*Lab maj 344 (16.1%)*
Catherine Smart	*LDm*	840	39.4%	
Ann Watkins	*Con*	109	5.1%	

May 1998 — *LDm gain from Lab*

2. Catherine Smart	*LDm*	1027	48.8%	*LDm maj 140 (6.7%)*
Paul Gilchrist	*Lab*	887	42.1%	
Hamish Downer	*Gre*	114	5.4%	
Peter Whitehead	*Con*	77	3.7%	

May 1999 — *No change*

3. Paul Gilchrist	*Lab*	1015	50.2%	*Lab maj 126 (6.2%)*
Jane Tienne	*LDm*	889	43.9%	
Vivian Ellis	*Con*	119	5.9%	

May 2000 — *LDm gain from Lab*

1. Sarah Ellis-Miller	*LDm*	951	45.0%	*LDm maj 51 (2.4%)*
Adrian Lucas (R)	*Lab*	900	42.6%	
Vivian Ellis	*Con*	134	6.3%	
Robert Milsom	*Gre*	126	5.4%	

May 2002 — *No change*

2. Catherine Smart (R)	*LDm*	969	44.8%	*LDm maj 102 (4.7%)*
Paul Sales	*Lab*	867	40.1%	
Vicky Russell	*Gre*	194	9.0%	
Vivian Ellis	*Con*	131	6.1%	

Romsey (contd.)

May 2003				*LDm gain from Lab*
3. Iain Coleman	*LDm*	892	43.8%	*LDm maj 103 (5.1%)*
Paul Gilchrist (R)	*Lab*	789	38.8%	
Vicky Russell	*Gre*	146	7.2%	
Richard Normington	*Con*	145	7.1%	
Diana Minns	*SoA*	63	3.1%	

General re-warding: Romsey gained Greville Road and William Smith Close from Coleridge.

June 2004 (All up election – 3 vacancies)				*3 LDm*
2. Catherine Smart (R)	*LDm*	1192	48.3%	
1. Iain Coleman (R)	*LDm*	1184	48.0%	
3. Sarah Ellis-Miller (R)	*LDm*	1125	45.6%	*LDm maj 379 (15.4%)*
Jonathan Goodacre	*Lab*	746	30.2%	
Paul Sales	*Lab*	658	26.7%	
Benjamin Stafford	*Lab*	577	23.4%	
Richard Rippin	*Gre*	394	16.0%	
Vicky Russell	*Gre*	360	14.6%	
Vivian Ellis	*Con*	206	8.3%	
Margaret Reynolds	*Con*	186	7.5%	
Rosemary Wheeler	*Con*	172	7.0%	
Marjorie Barr	*UKIP*	119	4.8%	

May 2006 (2 vacancies)				*No change*
3. Sarah Ellis-Miller (R)	*LDm*	1065	44.8%	
1. Raj Shah	*LDm*	815	34.3%	*LDm maj 192 (8.1%)*
Jonathan Goodacre	*Lab*	623	26.2%	
Tariq Sadiq	*Lab*	491	20.6%	
Jesse Griffiths	*Gre*	358	15.0%	
Thomas Woodcock	*Rsp*	294	12.4%	
Samuel Caldwell	*Rsp*	268	11.3%	
Hugh Mennie	*Con*	235	9.9%	
Neil Hewett	*Gre*	216	9.1%	
Angela Ozturk	*Con*	216	9.1%	

May 2007				*No change*
1. Raj Shah (R)	*LDm*	774	36.2%	*LDm maj 278 (13.0%)*
Jonathan Goodacre	*Lab*	496	23.2%	
Thomas Woodcock	*Rsp*	358	16.8%	
Jesse Griffiths	*Gre*	271	12.7%	
Angela Ozturk	*Con*	238	11.1%	

Romsey (contd.)

May 2008				*No change*
2. Catherine Smart (R)	*LDm*	791	37.2%	*LDm maj 256 (12.0%)*
Leonard Freeman	*Lab*	535	25.1%	
Thomas Woodcock	*LfL*	328	15.4%	
Samuel Barker	*Con*	285	13.4%	
Keith Garrett	*Gre*	189	8.9%	
May 2010				*No change*
3. Paul Saunders	*LDm*	1615	38.1%	*LDm maj 687 (16.2%)*
Edward Carlsson Browne	*Lab*	928	21.9%	
Hannah Allum	*Gre*	697	16.4%	
Jane Slinn	*Con*	600	14.1%	
Thomas Woodcock	*Soc*	404	9.5%	
May 2011				*Lab gain from LDm*
1. Zoe Moghadas	*Lab*	996	33.3%	*Lab maj 126 (4.2%)*
Raj Shah (R)	*LDm*	870	29.1%	
Jamie Gibson	*Gre*	411	13.7%	
Samuel Barker	*Con*	360	12.0%	
Thomas Woodcock	*Soc*	356	11.9%	
May 2012				*No change*
2. Catherine Smart (R)	*LDm*	1020	41.4%	*LDm maj 207 (8.4%)*
Rachel Eckersley	*Lab*	813	33.0%	
Thomas Woodcock	*Soc*	457	18.5%	
Philip Salway	*Con*	175	7.1%	
May 2014				*Lab gain from LDm*
3. Dave Baigent	*Lab*	1205	41.6%	*Lab maj 112 (3.9%)*
Paul Saunders (R)	*LDm*	1093	37.7%	
Megan Parry	*Gre*	394	13.6%	
Simon Lee	*Con*	206	7.1%	
May 2015				*No change*
1. Anna Smith	*Lab*	1636	37.7%	*Lab maj 322 (7.4%)*
Donald Adey	*LDm*	1314	30.3%	
Jane Carpenter	*Gre*	951	21.9%	
Rahatul Raja	*Con*	436	10.1%	

Romsey (contd.)

May 2016				Lab gain from LDm
2. Sophie Barnett	*Lab*	1409	49.7%	*Lab maj 393 13.9%*
Catherine Smart (R)	*LDm*	1016	35.8%	
Jane Carpenter	*Gre*	273	9.6%	
Roy Barton	*Con*	139	4.9%	

May 2018				No change
3. Dave Baigent (R)	*Lab*	1461	59.3%	*Lab maj 898 (36.5%)*
Joshua Blanchard Lewis	*LDm*	563	22.9%	
Caitlin Patterson	*Gre*	269	10.9%	
Martin Keegan	*Con*	170	6.9%	

May 2019				No change
1. Anna Smith (R)	*Lab*	1138	48.4%	*Lab maj 598 (25.4%)*
Caitlin Patterson	*Gre*	540	23.0%	
Joshua Blanchard Lewis	*LDm*	526	22.4%	
Martin Keegan	*Con*	146	6.2%	

No elections in 2020 due to Covid-19 pandemic

General re-warding (see map, near end of book)

May 2021 (All up elections – 3 vacancies)				3 Lab
1. Dave Baigent (R)	*Lab*	1575	52.3%	
2. Mairead Healey	*Lab*	1423	47.3%	
3. Dinah Pounds	*Lab*	1378	45.8%	*Lab maj 735 (24.4%)*
Sarah Nicmanis	*Gre*	643	21.4%	
Suzie Webb	*Gre*	632	21.0%	
Elisabeth Whitebread	*Gre*	615	20.4%	
Laura Ryan	*LDm*	526	17.5%	
Friso De Graaf	*LDm*	406	13.5%	
John Walmsley	*LDm*	375	12.5%	
Mohammed Azamuddin	*Con*	337	11.2%	
Daniel Collis	*Con*	332	11.0%	
Richard Haddon	*Con*	248	8.2%	

May 2022				No change
3. Dinah Pounds (R)	*Lab*	1548	58.1%	*Lab maj 1062 (39.8%)*
Suzie Webb	*Gre*	486	18.2%	
John Walmsley	*LDm*	416	15.6%	
Paul Roper	*Con*	215	8.1%	

Romsey (contd.)

May 2023 *No change*
2.Mairéad Healy (R)   *Lab*   1219   45.5%   *Lab maj 664 (24.8%)*
Suzie Webb   *Gre*   555   20.7%
Mohammed Azamuddin   *Con*   514   19.2%
John Walmsley   *LDm*   389   14.5%

May 2024 *No change*
1.Dave Baigent (R)   *Lab*   1433   52.2%   *Lab maj 909 (33.1%)*
Iain Webb   *Gre*   524   19.1%
John Walmsley   *LDm*   307   11.2%
Will Bannell   *Ind*   273   9.9%
Rob Nelson   *Con*   208   7.6%

September 2024 (byelection) *No change*
2.Beth Gardiner-Smith   *Lab*   596   42.8%   *Lab maj 187 (13.4%)*
Zak Karimjee   *Gre*   409   29.4%
John Walmsley   *LDm*   249   17.9%
Robert Nelson   *Con*   138   9.9%

2025 Dave Baigent left Lab to join YP

May 2026 *Gre gain*
Jacqui Whitmore   *Gre*   1521   45.2%   *Gre maj 397 (11.8%)*
Rosy Greenlees   *Lab*   1124   33.4%
John Walmsley   *LDm*   347   10.3%
Andrew Watson   *Rfm*   230   6.8%
Rob Nelson   *Con*   141   4.2%

~~~ St Matthew's ~~~

November 1935   (All up elections - 3 vacancies)   *2 Lab, Con*

1. Alex Wood (R)	*Lab*	793	51.3%	
3. Albert Stubbs (R)	*Lab*	730	47.2%	
2. Jesse Harwood	*Con*	727	47.0%	*Con maj (46 3.0%)* (R) St Andrews
Marcus D. Bradford	*Con*	681	44.0%	(R) St Andrews
Esther Foister (R)	*Lab*	673	43.5%	
Constance Wooten	*Con*	650	42.0%	(R) St Andrews

November 1936   *No change*

2. Jesse Harwood (R)	*Con*	740	53.2%	*Con maj 89 (6.4%)*
David Hardman	*Lab*	651	46.8%	

November 1937   *No change*

3. Albert Stubbs (R)	*Lab*	798	51.3%	*Lab maj 41 (2.6%)*
Sidney Rolfe	*Con*	757	48.7%	

November 1938   *No change*

Alex Wood (R)	*Lab*	unopposed

No elections held during World War II. John Overton co-opted.

November 1945 (2 vacancies)   *Lab gain from Con*

2. W.Donald Chapman	*Lab*	1178	64.4%	
1. John Overton (R)	*Lab*	1109	60.7%	*Lab maj 394 (21.6%)*
Hubert Woodley Betts	*Con*	715	39.1%	
Frank Pointer	*Con*	654	35.8%	

December 1945 (byelection)   *No change*

3. Arthur Cross	*Lab*	879	55.4%	*Lab maj 170 (10.7%)*
Sidney Rolfe	*Con*	709	44.6%	

November 1946   *No change*

1. John Overton (R)	*Lab*	1055	53.6%	*Lab maj 142 (7.2%)*
William Hardesty	*Con*	913	46.4%	

November 1947   *Con gain from Lab*

2. William Hardesty	*Con*	1270	50.1%	*Con maj 6 (0.2%)*
W.Donald Chapman (R)	*Lab*	1264	49.9%	

St Matthew's   (contd.)

May 1949				*Con gain from Lab*
3. Derek Traylen	*Con*	1293	54.6%	*Con maj 220 (9.3%)*
Leonard Wordingham	*Lab*	1073	45.4%	
May 1950				*Con gain from Lab*
1. Albert Cox	*Con*	1056	54.2%	*Con maj 163 (8.4%)*
John Overton (R)	*Lab*	893	45.8%	
May 1951				*No change*
2. William Hardesty (R)	*Con*	unopposed		
May 1952				*Lab gain from Con*
3. Geoffrey Baker	*Lab*	1145	51.0%	*Lab maj 44 (2.0%)*
Derek Traylen (R)	*Con*	1101	49.0%	
May 1953				*No change*
1. Albert Cox (R)	*Con*	962	51.4%	*Con maj 53 (2.8%)*
Frank Bailey	*Lab*	909	48.6%	
May 1954				*Lab gain from Con*
2. Frank Bailey	*Lab*	959	50.5%	*Lab maj 19 (1.0%)*
William Hardesty (R)	*Con*	940	49.5%	
May 1955				*Con gain from Lab*
3. William Hardesty	*Con*	1038	55.3%	*Con maj 200 (10.7%)*
Geoffrey Baker (R)	*Lab*	838	44.7%	
May 1956				*Lab gain from Con*
1. Raymond Flack	*Lab*	779	46.2%	*Lab maj 208 (12.3%)*
Albert Cox (R)	*Con*	571	33.9%	
Francis Leach	*RPA*	335	19.9%	
May 1957				*No change*
2. Frank Bailey (R)	*Lab*	920	54.0%	*Lab maj 136 (8.0%)*
Derek Traylen	*Con*	784	46.0%	
May 1958				*Lab gain from Con*
3. Florence Roden	*Lab*	840	52.8%	*Lab maj 88 (5.5%)*
William Hardesty (R)	*Con*	752	47.2%	

St Matthew's   (contd.)

May 1959				*Con gain from Lab*
1. William Hardesty	*Con*	729	51.2%	*Con maj 34 (2.4%)*
Raymond Flack (R)	*Lab*	695	48.8%	

May 1960				*Con gain from Lab*
2. Derek Traylen	*Con*	677	52.6%	*Con maj 66 (5.1%)*
Frank Bailey (R)	*Lab*	611	47.4%	

May 1961				*Con gain from Lab*
3. Brian Lister	*Con*	746	58.9%	*Con maj 225 (17.8%)*
Florence Roden (R)	*Lab*	521	41.1%	

May 1962				*Lab gain from Con*
1. Sonia Abrams	*Lab*	603	51.7%	*Lab maj 39 (3.3%)*
William Hardesty (R)	*Con*	564	48.3%	

May 1963				*Lab gain from Con*
2. Clarissa Kaldor	*Lab*	656	50.5%	*Lab maj 12 (0.9%)*
Derek Traylen (R)	*Con*	644	49.5%	

May 1964				*Lab gain from Con*
3. Josef Schicker	*Lab*	658	58.0%	*Lab maj 181 (15.9%)*
Peter John	*Con*	477	42.0%	

May 1965				*No change*
1. Sonia Abrams (R)	*Lab*	unopposed		

May 1966				*No change*
2. Clarissa Kaldor (R)	*Lab*	unopposed		

November 1966 (byelection)				*Ind gain from Lab*
1. Rev.Victor Dixon	*Ind*	392	39.8%	*Ind maj 73 (7.4%)*
Frank Ramsbottom	*Lab*	319	32.4%	
Helga Howard	*Con*	273	27.7%	

May 1967				*Con gain from Lab*
3. Anthony Cornell	*Con*	447	41.0%	*Con maj 118 (10.8%)*
Josef Schicker (R)	*Lab*	329	30.2%	
David Murray	*Lib*	313	28.7%	

In 1968 St Matthew's Ward was abolished and the sitting councillors assigned to the newly formed Arbury Ward.

~~~ **Trumpington** ~~~

November 1935   (All up elections - 3 vacancies)   *2 Ind, WCA*

1.Arthur Dilley	*Ind*	1013	71.4%	(R) Cambridge Without
3. Ernest Peck	*Ind*	675	47.6%	(R) Fitzwilliam
2. Eva Hartree	*WCA*	606	42.7%	*WCA maj 51 (3.6%)* (R)*
Edwin Jackson	*Ind*	555	39.1%	(R) New Town
Harold Woor	*Con*	379	26.7%	
Frederick Blott (R)	*Con*	291	20.5%	(R) New Town

(* Eva Hartree (R) South Chesterton)

November 1936   *No change*

2. Eva Hartree (R)   *WCA*   unopposed

November 1937   *No change*

3. Ernest Peck (R)   *Ind*   unopposed

November 1938   *No change*

1. Arthur Dilley (R)   *Ind*   unopposed

December 1938 (byelection)   *No change*

3. Lucy Cooke (R)   *Ind*   unopposed

No elections held during World War II.   Stewart Bull co-opted

November 1945 (2 vacancies)   *Con gain from Ind, Lab gain from Ind*

1. Walter Light	*Con*	821	45.5%	
3. Edward Andrews	*Lab*	792	43.9%	*Lab maj 61 (3.4%)*
Stewart Bull (R)	*Ind*	731	40.5%	
Sybil Hutton	*Ind*	720	39.9%	
Pearl Lilley	*Comm*	543	30.1%	

November 1946   *Con gain from WCA*

2. C.Elliot Ridgeon	*Con*	1111	54.9%	*Con maj 608 (30.1%)*
Sybil Hutton	*Ind*	503	24.9%	
Pearl Lilley	*Comm*	409	20.2%	

November 1947   *Con gain from Lab*

3. Henry Naylor	*Con*	1547	66.3%	*Con maj 761 (32.6%)*
Edward Andrews (R)	*Lab*	786	33.7%	

May 1949				*No change*
1. Leslie Jackson	*Con*	1459	61.1%	*Con maj 579 (24.3%)*
Douglas Bassett	*Lab*	880	36.9%	
Jane Woolstencroft	*Comm*	47	2.0%	

May 1950				*No change*
2. C.Elliot Ridgeon (R)	*Con*	1436	66.7%	*Con maj 720 (33.5%)*
John Clark	*Lab*	716	33.3%	

May 1951				*No change*
3. Lilian Thomson	*Con*	unopposed		

May 1952				*No change*
1. Leslie Jackson (R)	*Con*	unopposed		

May 1953				*No change*
2. C.Elliot Ridgeon (R)	*Con*	1299	61.4%	*Con maj 481 (22.7%)*
Denis Ash	*Lab*	818	38.6%	

May 1954				*No change*
3. Lilian Thomson (R)	*Con*	unopposed		

May 1955				*No change*
1. Leslie Jackson (R)	*Con*	unopposed		

May 1956				*No change*
2. C.Elliot Ridgeon (R)	*Con*	1089	47.1%	*Con maj 248 (10.7%)*
Thomas Carr	*Lab*	841	36.3%	
Derek Tozer	*RPA*	384	16.6%	

May 1957				*No change*
3. Mabel Morse	*Con*	1154	53.1%	*Con maj 134 (6.2%)*
Thomas Carr	*Lab*	1020	46.9%	

May 1958				*No change*
1. Leslie Jackson (R)	*Con*	1279	61.2%	*Con maj 467 (22.3%)*
James Challis	*Lab*	812	38.8%	

May 1959				*No change*
2. Harry Woolgar	*Con*	1259	66.4%	*Con maj 623 (32.9%)*
William Hughes	*ILP*	636	33.6%	

Trumpington   (contd.)

May 1960 *No change*
3. Mabel Morse (R) *Con* 1117 61.3% *Con maj 411 (22.5%)*
William Hughes *Lab* 706 38.7%

May 1961 *No change*
1. Leslie Jackson (R) *Con* unopposed

May 1962 *No change*
2. Harry Woolgar (R) *Con* 998 55.4% *Con maj 196 (10.9%)*
Doris Howe *Lab* 802 44.6%

May 1963 (2 vacancies) *No change*
3. Mabel Morse (R) *Con* 1041 59.8%
2. Jean Barker *Con* 1004 57.7% *Con maj 284 (16.3%)*
Philip Abrams *Lab* 720 41.4%
Doris Howe *Lab* 716 41.1%

July 1963 (byelection) *No change*
1. Robert Wright *Con* 652 40.3% *Con maj 120 (7.4%)*
Tom Dale *Lib* 532 32.9%
Paul Rayment *Lab* 433 26.8%

May 1964 *No change*
1. Robert Wright (R) *Con* 1073 57.3% *Con maj 275 (14.7%)*
Elizabeth Hudson *Lab* 798 42.7%

May 1965 *No change*
2. Jean Barker (R) *Con* unopposed

May 1966 *No change*
3. Mabel Morse (R) *Con* unopposed

May 1967 *No change*
1. Robert Wright (R) *Con* unopposed

General re-warding: Trumpington was unaffected.

May 1968 *No change*
2. Jean Barker (R) *Con* 1044 77.5% *Con maj 741 (55.0%)*
David Keate *Lab* 303 22.5%

Trumpington   (contd.)

May 1969				*No change*
3. Mabel Morse (R)	*Con*	1063	80.7%	*Con maj 808 (61.3%)*
Michael Fuller	*Lab*	255	19.3%	

May 1970				*No change*
1. Robert Wright (R)	*Con*	1144	66.9%	*Con maj 578 (33.8%)*
O.M.Wendy Nicol	*Lab*	566	33.1%	

September 1970 (byelection)				*No change*
3. Gordon Rolfe	*Con*	841	67.1%	*Con maj 428 (34.1%)*
Robert Woods	*Lab*	413	32.9%	

May 1971				*No change*
2. Jean Barker (R)	*Con*	1183	56.2%	*Con maj 261 (12.4%)*
Elizabeth Peel	*Lab*	922	43.8%	

May 1972				*No change*
3. Gordon Rolfe (R)	*Con*	1178	55.9%	*Con maj 249 (11.8%)*
Elizabeth Peel	*Lab*	929	44.1%	

June 1973 (All up elections – 3 vacancies, all retiring 1976)				*3 Con*
Robert Wright (R)	*Con*	942	58.2%	
Gordon Rolfe (R)	*Con*	901	55.6%	
Millicent Suckling	*Con*	858	53.0%	*Con maj 44 (2.7%)*
Kathleen Gardiner	*Lab*	814	50.3%	
Mary Tucker	*Lab*	678	41.9%	
Joseph Chamberlain	*Lab*	666	41.1%	

General re-warding: Trumpington gained the area between Hills Road and the railway, from Coleridge and Cherry Hinton.

May 1976 (All up elections – 3 vacancies)				*3 Con*
1. Robert Wright (R)	*Con*	1511	66.0%	
3. Beryl Harrison	*Con*	1453	63.5%	
2. Millicent Suckling (R)	*Con*	1447	63.2%	*Con maj 710 (31.0%)*
Sally Richer	*Lab*	737	32.2%	

May 1978				*No change*
2. Millicent Suckling (R)	*Con*	1406	62.1%	*Con maj 882 (38.9%)*
Stephen Watts	*Lab*	524	23.1%	
David Green	*Lib*	287	12.7%	
David Mourton	*Comm*	48	2.1%	

Trumpington   (contd.)

July 1978 (byelection)				*No change*
3. Elaine Wheatley	*Con*	1053	56.9%	*Con maj 441 (23.8%)*
Stephen Watts	*Lab*	612	33.1%	
David Green	*Lib*	146	7.9%	
David Mourton	*Comm*	39	2.1%	

May 1979				*No change*
3. Elaine Wheatley (R)	*Con*	2019	51.9%	*Con maj 952 (24.5%)*
Stephen Watts	*Lab*	1067	27.4%	
David Green	*Lib*	747	19.2%	
David Mourton	*Comm*	59	1.5%	

May 1980				*No change*
1. Robert Wright (R)	*Con*	1226	56.5%	*Con maj 628 (29.0%)*
Stephen Watts	*Lab*	598	27.6%	
John Walker	*Lib*	345	15.9%	

May 1982				*No change*
2. Millicent Suckling (R)	*Con*	1409	55.6%	*Con maj 691 (27.3%)*
Kevin Robinson	*SDP*	718	28.4%	
Stephen Pugh	*Lab*	405	16.0%	

May 1983				*No change*
3. Elaine Wheatley (R)	*Con*	1428	58.0%	*Con maj 883 (35.9%)*
Kevin Robinson	*SDP*	545	22.1%	
Alyson Makin	*Lab*	488	19.8%	

May 1984				*No change*
1. Geoffrey Clark	*Con*	1166	49.4%	*Con maj 399 (16.9%)*
Anne Kent	*SDP*	767	32.5%	
Alyson Makin	*Lab*	427	18.1%	

May 1986				*No change*
2. Millicent Suckling (R)	*Con*	1374	48.5%	*Con maj 399 (16.9%)*
Philippa Slatter	*SDP*	994	35.1%	
Nicola Glegg	*Lab*	438	15.5%	
Lewis Wilbur	*Ind*	26	0.9%	

May 1987				*No change*
3. Elaine Wheatley (R)	*Con*	1495	51.1%	*Con maj 454 (15.5%)*
Philippa Slatter	*SDP*	1041	35.6%	
Martin Rose	*Lab*	387	13.2%	

Trumpington   (contd.)

May 1988				*No change*
1. Sonja Froggett	*Con*	1255	51.8%	*Con maj 508 (21.0%)*
Philippa Slatter	*SLD*	747	30.8%	
Andrew Robson	*Lab*	420	17.3%	

November 1988 (byelection)				*No change*
2. Margaret Hoskins	*Con*	967	52.5%	*Con maj 301 (16.3%)*
Philippa Slatter	*SLD*	666	36.2%	
Andrew Robson	*Lab*	208	11.3%	

May 1990				*No change*
2. Margaret Hoskins (R)	*Con*	1151	40.7%	*Con maj 438 (15.5%)*
Andrew Powell	*Lab*	713	25.2%	
Philippa Slatter	*LDm*	708	25.0%	
David Rees	*Gre*	255	9.0%	

May 1991				*No change*
3. Justin Coleman	*Con*	1235	48.9%	*Con maj 553 (21.9%)*
Philippa Slatter	*LDm*	682	27.0%	
Andrew Powell	*Lab*	469	18.6%	
David Rees	*Gre*	139	5.5%	

May 1992				*No change*
1. Sonja Froggett (R)	*Con*	1283	56.2%	*Con maj 650 (28.5%)*
Philippa Slatter	*LDm*	633	27.8%	
Christopher Wilson	*Lab*	365	16.0%	

May 1994				*LDm gain from Con*
2. Stephen Warde	*LDm*	1201	46.2%	*LDm maj 206 (7.9%)*
Margaret Hoskins (R)	*Con*	995	38.3%	
Colin Dickins	*Lab*	402	15.5%	

May 1995				*LDm gain from Con*
3. Philippa Slatter	*LDm*	1056	45.2%	*LDm maj 254 (10.9%)*
Margaret Hoskins	*Con*	802	34.3%	
Robert Hardy	*Lab*	480	20.5%	

May 1996				*LDm gain from Con*
1. Hazel Eagle	*LDm*	886	41.2%	*LDm maj 71 (3.3%)*
Sonja Froggett (R)	*Con*	815	37.9%	
Kira Davison	*Lab*	447	20.8%	

Trumpington   (contd.)

May 1998				*Con gain from LDm*
2. Donald Douglas	*Con*	910	45.0%	*Con maj 91 (4.5%)*
Michael Dixon	*LDm*	819	40.5%	
Patrick Diamond	*Lab*	294	14.5%	

May 1999				*No change*
3. Philippa Slatter (R)	*LDm*	1205	52.2%	*LDm maj 268 (11.6%)*
Elaine Wheatley	*Con*	937	40.6%	
Denstone Kemp	*Lab*	168	7.3%	

May 2000				*No change*
1. Jean Currie	*LDm*	1096	49.0%	*LDm maj 171 (7.6%)*
Fiona McNish	*Con*	925	41.4%	
Maria Bell	*Lab*	216	9.7%	

May 2002				*LDm gain from Con*
2. Judith Pinnington	*LDm*	1118	47.5%	*LDm maj 181 (7.7%)*
Hannah Towns	*Con*	937	39.8%	
Rosemary Turner	*Lab*	201	8.5%	
Brian Westcott	*Gre*	100	4.2%	

May 2003 (2 vacancies)				*No change*
3. Philippa Slatter (R)	*LDm*	1225	50.4%	
2. Edrich Adigun-Harris	*LDm*	1126	46.4%	*LDm maj 177 (7.3%)*
Hannah Towns	*Con*	949	39.1%	
Steven George	*Con*	914	37.6%	
Neil Ford	*Gre*	181	7.5%	
David Coulson	*Lab*	150	6.2%	
Jonathan Goodacre	*Lab*	135	5.6%	

General re-warding: Trumpington lost the area between Hills Road and the railway line to Queen Edith's and Coleridge and gained areas south of Fenner's and Station Road from Petersfield and Lensfield Road from Market.

Trumpington   (contd.)

June 2004 (All up election – 3 vacancies)				*3 LDm*
2. Philippa Slatter (R)	*LDm*	1186	51.8%	
1. Edrich Adigun-Harris (R) *LDm*		1177	51.4%	
3. Sheila Churchill *	*LDm*	1039	45.4%	*LDm maj 261 (11.4%)*
Steven George	*Con*	778	34.0%	
Andre Beaumont	*Con*	764	33.3%	
Daniel Whant	*Con*	679	29.6%	
Ceri Galloway	*Gre*	346	15.1%	
Deborah Allen	*Lab*	192	8.4%	
George Tudor	*Lab*	162	7.1%	
David Coulson	*Lab*	154	6.7%	

(* Sheila Churchill became Sheila Stuart in 2005)

May 2006				*No change*
3. Sheila Stuart (R)	*LDm*	960	45.5%	*LDm maj 208 (9.9%)*
John Ionides	*Con*	752	35.7%	
Ceri Galloway	*Gre*	205	9.7%	
Pamela Stacey	*Lab*	191	9.1%	

November 2006 (byelection)				*No change*
1. Andrew Blackhurst	*LDm*	858	51.4%	*LDm maj 240 (14.4%)*
John Ionides	*Con*	618	37.0%	
Pamela Stacey	*Lab*	109	6.5%	
Ceri Galloway	*Gre*	85	5.1%	

May 2007				*No change*
1. Andrew Blackhurst (R) *LDm*		913	45.2%	*LDm maj 139 (6.9%)*
Peter Hase	*Con*	774	38.3%	
Ceri Galloway	*Gre*	172	8.5%	
Pamela Stacey	*Lab*	160	7.9%	

May 2008				*No change*
2. Salah Al Bander	*LDm*	985	45.9%	*LDm maj 157 (7.3%)*
Peter Hase	*Con*	828	38.6%	
Ceri Galloway	*Gre*	178	8.3%	
Pamela Stacey	*Lab*	154	7.2%	

May 2010				*No change*
3. Sheila Stuart (R)	*LDm*	1704	43.2%	*LDm maj 468 (11.9%)*
Julie Simpole-Clarke	*Con*	1236	31.3%	
Kenny Latunde-Dada	*Lab*	559	14.2%	
Ceri Galloway	*Gre*	446	11.3%	

Trumpington   (contd.)

May 2011   *No change*

1. Andrew Blackhurst (R) *LDm* 991   36.1%   *LDm maj 122 (4.4%)*
John Ionides   *Con*   869   31.7%
Kenny Latunde-Dada   *Lab*   481   17.5%
Ceri Galloway   *Gre*   401   14.6%

May 2012   *Con gain from LDm*

2. Shapour Meftah   *Con*   723   36.6%   *Con maj 79 (4.0%)*
Salah Al Bander (R)   *LDm*   644   32.6%
Kenny Latunde-Dada   *Lab*   321   16.3%
Ceri Galloway   *Gre*   287   14.5%

May 2014   *No change*

3. Nicholas Avery   *LDm*   1066   38.9%   LDm maj 264 (9.6%)
Richard Jeffs   *Con*   802   29.3%
Tim Sykes   *Lab*   440   16.1%
Ceri Galloway   *Gre*   429   15.7%

May 2015   *No change*

1. Zoe O'Connell   *LDm*   1498   29.9%   *LDm maj 132 (2.6%)*
Daniel John   *Con*   1366   27.3%
Nick Gay   *Lab*   1182   23.6%
Ceri Galloway   *Gre*   751   15.0%
Richard Jeffs   *UKIP*   213   4.3%

May 2016   *LDm gain from Con*

2. Donald Adey   *LDm* *   1212   41.3%   *LDm maj 457 (15.6%)*
Nick Gay   *Lab*   755   25.7%
Shapour Meftah (R)   *Con*   664   22.6%
Ceri Galloway   *Gre*   305   10.4%
(* *Donald Adey sat as an Independent from 2018*)

August 2022 (byelection)   *No change*

1. David Levien   *LDm*   1017   49.8%   LDm maj 545 (26.7%)
Rahimma Ahammed   *Lab*   472   23.1%
Ceri Galloway   *Gre*   298   14.6%
Shapour Meftah   *Con*   256   12.5%

Trumpington   (contd.)

May 2018   *Lab gain from LDm*

3. Katie Thornburrow	*Lab*	1302	37.7%	*Lab maj 4 (0.1%)*
Dan Hilken	*LDm*	1298	37.6%	
Phil Salway	*Con*	561	16.2%	
Ceri Galloway	*Gre*	293	8.5%	

May 2019 (2 vacancies)   *1 LDm gain from Ind*

1. Peter Lord	*LDm*	1509	43.2%	
2. Leo Summerbell	*LDm*	1474	42.2%	*LDm maj 497 (14.2%)*
Matt Bird	*Lab*	977	27.9%	
May Shafi	*Lab*	773	22.1%	
Ceri Galloway	*Gre*	600	17.2%	
Shapour Meftah	*Con*	431	12.3%	
Sue Wells	*Gre*	399	11.4%	
Philip James	*Con*	349	10.0%	

No elections in 2020 due to Covid-19 pandemic

General re-warding (see map, near end of book)

May 2021 (All up elections – 3 vacancies)   *3 LDm*

1. Alan Cox	*LDm*	1298	40.4%	
2. Ingrid Flaubert	*LDm*	1246	38.7%	
3. Olaf Hauk	*LDm*	1085	33.7%	*LDm maj 139 (4.3%)*
Amanda Hawkes	*Lab*	946	29.4%	
Nasir Uddin	*Lab*	729	22.7%	
Arran Parry-Davies	*Lab*	720	22.4%	
Ceri Galloway	*Gre*	604	18.8%	
Laurence Fischer	*Con*	574	17.8%	
Steven George	*Con*	548	17.0%	
Mike Spencer	*Con*	421	13.1%	
Sue Wells	*Gre*	359	11.2%	
Hero Tardrew	*Gre*	319	9.9%	

May 2022   *No change*

3. Olaf Hauk (R)	*LDm*	1151	42.1%	*LDm maj 298 (10.9%)*
Carlos Toranzos	*Lab*	853	31.2%	
Shapour Meftah	*Con*	379	13.9%	
Ceri Galloway	*Gre*	352	12.9%	

Trumpington   (contd.)

May 2023   *No change*

2.Ingrid Flaubert (R)	*LDm*	931	35.6%	*LDm maj 179 (6.8%)*
Carlos Toranzos	*Lab*	752	28.8%	
Shapour Meftah	*Con*	605	23.1%	
Chloe Mosonyi	*Gre*	327	12.5%	

May 2024   *No change*

1.Nadya Lokhmotova	LDm	944	36.4%	*LDm maj 179 (6.8%)*
Carlos Toranzos	Lab	836	32.3%	
Steven George	Con	481	18.6%	
Chloé Mosonyi	Gre	331	12.8%	

2026 - Ingrid Flaubert left LDm to join Gre

May 2026 (2 vacancies)   *No change*

3. Olaf Hauk (R)	*LDm*	1272	40.1%	*LDm maj 294 (9.3%)*
2. John Grimwood	*LDm*	1148	36.2%	
Edward Gokmen	*Gre*	854	26.9%	
Chloë Mosonyi	*Gre*	772	24.3%	
Carlos Toranzos	*Lab*	477	15.0%	
Henry Shailer	*Lab*	444	14.0%	
Steven George	*Con*	397	12.5%	
Guy Greenway	*Rfm*	293	9.2%	
John Ionides	*Con*	283	8.9%	
Samuel Lloyd	*Rfm*	275	8.7%	

~~~ **West Chesterton** ~~~

November 1935   (All up elections - 3 vacancies)   *2 Con, Ind*

1. Sidney Taylor	*Con*	1043	54.0%	(R) North Chesterton
3. Sidney Stokes	*Con*	915	47.4%	
2. Robert Hensher	*Ind*	865	44.8%	*Ind maj 229 (11.9%)* (R) *
I.C. Cash	*Con*	636	33.0%	
Edward Burgess	*Lab*	565	29.3%	
C. Wilkinson	*ILP*	495	25.6%	
Mrs Meldrum	*Lab*	491	25.4%	

(* Robert Hensher (R) North Chesterton)

November 1936   *Con gain from Ind*

2. Harry Langdon	*Con*	638	39.3%	*Con maj 8 (0.5%)*
Irene Stevens	*?*	630	38.8%	
Edward Burgess	*Lab*	355	21.9%	

November 1937   *No change*

| **3. Sidney Stokes** (R) | *Con* | 726 | 55.4% | *Con maj 141 (10.8%)* |
| Claude Stevenson | *Ind* | 585 | 44.6% | |

November 1938   *No change*

| **1. Sidney Taylor** (R) | *Con* | unopposed | | |

No elections held during World War II. George Nobbs co-opted

November 1945 (2 vacancies)   *No change*

2. George Nobbs (R)	*Con*	1447	70.9%	
1. Henry Langdon (R)	*Con*	1426	69.9%	*Con maj 219 (10.7%)*
Frederick Broad	*Lab*	1207	59.2%	

November 1946   *No change*

3. Horace Lister	*Con*	1719	50.9%	*Con maj 623 (18.4%).*
Frederick Broad	*Lab*	1096	32.4%	
Percy King	*Ind*	563	16.7%	

November 1947   *No change*

| **1. Henry Langdon** (R) | *Con* | 2447 | 68.5% | *Con maj 1324 (37.1%)* |
| Frederick Broad | *Lab* | 1123 | 31.5% | |

West Chesterton   (contd.)

May 1949 (2 vacancies)				*No change*
2. George Nobbs (R)	*Con*	2414	72.3%	
1. Horace Race	*Con*	2328	69.7%	*Con maj 1346 (40.3%)*
Ann Tweed	*Lab*	982	29.4%	
Phyllis Clark	*Lab*	955	28.6%	

May 1950 (2 vacancies)				*No change*
3. Arthur Halcrow	*Con*	2043	81.9%	
2. Harold De Ste Croix	*Con*	1943	77.9%	*Con maj 943 (37.8%)*
Ann Tweed	*Lab*	1000	40.1%	

May 1951			*No change*
1. Horace Race (R)	*Con*	unopposed	

May 1952			*No change*
2. Harold De Ste Croix (R) *Con*		unopposed	

May 1953				*No change*
3. Arthur Halcrow (R)	*Con*	1878	70.7%	*Con maj 1099 (41.4%)*
Stanley Ambrose	*Lab*	779	29.3%	

May 1954				*No change*
1. Horace Race (R)	*Con*	2010	95.6%	*Con maj 1918 (91.2%)*
M.Joan Jordan	*Comm*	92	4.4%	

May 1955				*No change*
2. Harold De Ste Croix (R) *Con*		2006	95.7%	*Con maj 1915 (91.3%)*
Ivor Jordan	*Comm*	91	4.3%	

May 1956				*No change*
3. Arthur Halcrow (R)	*Con*	1550	62.1%	*Con maj 604 (24.2%)*
Ann Tweed	*Lab*	946	37.9%	

May 1957				*No change*
1. Alec Gray	*Con*	1728	58.4%	*Con maj 498 (16.8%)*
Ann Tweed	*Lab*	1230	41.6%	

May 1958				*No change*
2. Percy Ginn	*Con*	1891	65.4%	*Con maj 889 (30.7%)*
Josef Schicker	*Lab*	1002	34.6%	

West Chesterton   (contd.)

May 1959				*No change*
3. Arthur Halcrow (R)	*Con*	1854	80.6%	*Con maj 1407 (61.1%)*
David Stovin	*ILP*	447	19.4%	

May 1960				*No change*
1. Alec Gray (R)	*Con*	1669	60.6%	*Con maj 584 (21.2%)*
Frank Ramsbottom	*Lab*	1085	39.4%	

May 1961				*No change*
2. Percy Ginn (R)	*Con*	1615	54.1%	*Con maj 246 (8.2%)*
Frank Ramsbottom	*Lab*	1369	45.9%	

May 1962				*No change*
3. Arthur Halcrow (R)	*Con*	1608	52.1%	*Con maj 127 (4.1%)*
Ann Tweed	*Lab*	1481	47.9%	

May 1963				*Lab gain from Con*
1. Ann Tweed	*Lab*	1713	40.5%	*Lab maj 408 (9.6%)*
Margaret Cook	*Lib*	1305	30.8%	
John Dickerson	*Con*	1215	28.7%	

December 1963 (byelection)				*Lab gain from Con*
3. Robert May	*Lab*	1054	37.4%	*Lab maj 45 (1.6%)*
Sidney Hopkins	*Con*	1009	35.8%	
Margaret Cook	*Lib*	752	26.7%	

May 1964				*No change*
2. Edward Oakden	*Con*	2256	50.6%	*Con maj 57 (1.3%)*
Frank Ramsbottom	*Lab*	2199	49.4%	

May 1965				*Con gain from Lab*
3. Gordon Budd	*Con*	2282	59.3%	*Con maj 715 (18.6%)*
Robert May (R)	*Lab*	1567	40.7%	

May 1966				*Con gain from Lab*
1. Maurice Garner	*Con*	2310	53.2%	*Con maj 279 (6.4%)*
Ann Tweed (R)	*Lab*	2031	46.8%	

May 1967				*No change*
2. Edward Oakden (R)	*Con*	2786	66.9%	*Con maj 1407 (33.8%)*
John Proud	*Lab*	1379	33.1%	

<h1 style="text-align:center">West Chesterton (contd.)</h1>

General re-warding: A new ward, Arbury, was created, mostly from West Chesteron, which gained area from East Chesterton.

May 1968 (2 vacancies)				*No change*
3. Percival Reed	*Con*	1398	80.0%	
2. John Pettitt	*Con*	1377	78.8%	*Con maj 1014 (58.0%)*
Leonard Freeman	*Lab*	363	20.8%	
Matthew Clark	*Lab*	359	20.5%	

May 1969				*No change*
1. Maurice Garner (R)	*Con*	1388	76.5%	*Con maj 962 (53.0%)*
Leonard Freeman	*Lab*	426	23.5%	

May 1970				*No change*
2. John Pettitt (R)	*Con*	1277	75.3%	*Con maj 858 (50.6%)*
Brian Shearey	*Lab*	419	24.7%	

May 1971				*No change*
3. Percival Reed (R)	*Con*	1227	57.0%	*Con maj 302 (14.0%)*
Kenneth Judge	*Lab*	925	43.0%	

May 1972				*No change*
1. Maurice Garner (R)	*Con*	1321	62.6%	*Con maj 531 (25.2%)*
Harold Nightingale	*Lab*	790	37.4%	

June 1973 (All up elections – 3 vacancies, all retiring 1976)				*3 Con*
Maurice Garner (R)	*Con*	1093	61.6%	
Percival Reed (R)	*Con*	1014	57.1%	
Chris Gough-Goodman	*Con*	983	55.4%	*Con maj 485 (27.3%)*
Harold Nightingale	*Lab*	498	28.1%	
Kenneth Judge	*Lab*	483	27.2%	
Bernard Silverman	*Lab*	445	25.1%	
Ruth Conolly	*Lib*	439	24.7%	
Terence Braverman	*Lib*	368	20.7%	

General re-warding: West Chesteron lost the area east of Elizabeth Way to East Chesterton; gained the area west of Gilbert Rd / Milton Rd / Victoria Ave from Castle and Newnham.

West Chesterton   (contd.)

May 1976 (All up elections – 3 vacancies)				*3 Cons*
1. Maurice Garner (R)	*Con*	1578	70.5%	
3. Percival Reed (R)	*Con*	1494	66.8%	
2. Chris Gough-Goodman (R)	*Con*	1461	65.3%	*Con maj 865 (38.7%)*
Julian Hunt	*Lab*	596	26.6%	
Harold Nightingale	*Lab*	562	25.1%	
Albert Lehmann	*Lab*	519	23.2%	

May 1978				*No change*
2. Chris Gough-Goodman (R)	*Con*	1284	66.7%	*Con maj 643 (33.4%)*
Richard Overy	*Lab*	641	33.3%	

May 1979				*No change*
3. Percival Reed (R)	*Con*	1827	49.9%	*Con maj 722 (19.7%)*
John Elliott	*Lab*	1105	30.2%	
Andrew Gore	*Lib*	726	19.8%	

May 1980				*No change*
1. Maurice Garner (R)	*Con*	1123	57.9%	*Con maj 591 (30.5%)*
Richard Wall	*Lab*	532	27.4%	
Anthony Waite	*Lib*	284	14.6%	

May 1982				*Lib gain from Con*
2. Mark Hayes	*Lib*	1126	41.5%	*Lib maj 1 (0.04%)*
Chris Gough-Goodman (R)	*Con*	1125	41.5%	
Anil Sinha	*Lab*	461	17.0%	

May 1983				*Lib gain from Con*
3. Hilary Richmond	*Lib*	1301	43.5%	*Lib maj 155 (5.2%)*
Percival Reed (R)	*Con*	1146	38.4%	
Anil Sinha	*Lab*	541	18.1%	

May 1984				*Lib gain from Con*
1. Simon Boyd	*Lib*	1206	41.7%	*Lib maj 138 (4.8%)*
Maurice Garner (R)	*Con*	1068	36.9%	
Richard Overy	*Lab*	617	21.3%	

May 1986				*No change*
2. Stephen Marshall	*SDP*	1043	36.6%	*SDP maj 37 (1.3%)*
James Strachan	*Con*	1006	35.3%	
Paul McHugh	*Lab*	664	23.3%	
Margaret Wright	*Gre*	134	4.7%	

<h1 style="text-align:center">West Chesterton   (contd.)</h1>

May 1987				*No change*
3. Evelyn Knowles	*SDP*	1416	43.9%	*SDP maj 161 (5.0%)*
James Strachan	*Con*	1255	38.9%	
Valerie Antopolski	*Lab*	552	17.1%	

May 1988				*Con gain from Lib*
1. James Strachan	*Con*	1074	39.1%	*Con maj 195 (7.1%)*
Margaret Trowell	*SLD*	879	32.0%	
Christine Mann	*Lab*	674	24.5%	
Margaret Wright	*Gre*	123	4.5%	

May 1990				*No change*
2. M.Ian Nimmo-Smith	*LDm*	992	31.6%	*LDm maj 11 (0.4%)*
Christine Mann	*Lab*	981	31.3%	
Rodney Stokes	*Con*	928	29.6%	
Margaret Wright	*Gre*	235	7.5%	

May 1991				*No change*
3. Evelyn Knowles (R)	*LDm*	1242	43.3%	*LDm maj 419 (14.6%)*
Paul McHugh	*Lab*	823	28.7%	
Michael Farrington	*Con*	803	28.0%	

May 1992				*LDm gain from Con*
1. Gaynor Griffiths	*LDm*	1008	37.7%	*LDm maj 130 (4.9%)*
Christine Mann	*Lab*	878	32.8%	
Sandra Manley	*Con*	787	29.4%	

May 1994				*No change*
2. M.Ian Nimmo-Smith (R)	*LDm*	1347	50.0%	*LDm maj 356 (13.2%)*
Paul Humber	*Lab*	991	36.8%	
Dianne Walton	*Con*	355	13.2%	

May 1995				*No change*
3. Evelyn Knowles (R)	*LDm*	1224	49.5%	*LDm maj 329 (13.3%)*
Christine Mann	*Lab*	895	36.2%	
Graham Stuart	*Con*	355	14.3%	

May 1996				*No change*
1. Gaynor Griffiths (R)	*LDm*	1221	53.1%	*LDm maj 466 (20.3%)*
Ben Wardle	*Lab*	755	32.8%	
Graham Stuart	*Con*	323	14.0%	

West Chesterton   (contd.)

May 1998   *No change*
2. M.Ian Nimmo-Smith (R) *LDm*   973   51.4%   *LDm maj 427 (22.5%)*
Patrick Schicker   *Lab*   546   28.8%
Vivian Ellis   *Con*   233   12.3%
Margaret Wright   *Gre*   142   7.5%

May 1999   *No change*
3. Evelyn Knowles (R)   *LDm*   872   49.3%   *LDm maj 369 (20.8%)*
Patrick Schicker   *Lab*   503   28.4%
Richard Hoile   *Con*   237   13.4%
Jennifer Ward   *Gre*   158   8.9%

May 2000   *No change*
1. Gaynor Griffiths (R) *LDm*   856   46.7%   *LDm maj 295 (16.1%)*
David Gosling   *Lab*   561   30.6%
Richard Hoile   *Con*   303   16.5%
Gerhard Goldbeck-Wood *Gre*   112   6.1%

May 2002   *No change*
2. M.Ian Nimmo-Smith (R) *LDm* 1071   51.1%   *LDm maj 597 (28.5%)*
Patrick Schicker   *Lab*   474   22.6%
James Strachan   *Con*   350   16.7%
Stephen Peake   *Gre*   202   9.6%

May 2003 (2 vacancies)   *No change*
3. R.A.Max Boyce   *LDm*   941   50.2%
2. Nichola Harrison   *LDm*   912   48.6%   *LDm maj 522 (27.8%)*   (R) *
L.Mick Brown   *Lab*   390   20.8%
Michael Sargeant   *Lab*   368   19.6%
James Strachan   *Con*   341   18.2%
Graham Palmer   *Con*   298   15.9%
Sarah Peake   *Gre*   233   12.4%
Stephen Peake   *Gre*   155   8.3%
(* Nichola Harrison (R) Newnham)

General re-warding: West Chesterton gained Bateson Road and both sides of Milton
Road.

West Chesterton (contd.)

June 2004				*No change*
2. M.Ian Nimmo-Smith (R)	*LDm*	1302	50.8%	
1. Diane Armstrong	*LDm*	1143	44.6%	
3. R.A.Max Boyce (R)	*LDm*	1086	42.3%	*LDm maj 583 (22.7%)*
Paul McHugh	*Lab*	503	19.6%	
Sarah Peake	*Gre*	481	18.8%	
Miriam Lynn	*Lab*	480	18.7%	
Peter Lake	*Con*	478	18.6%	
James Strachan	*Con*	463	18.1%	
Simon Watkins	*Lab*	454	17.7%	
Ann Watkins	*Con*	436	17.0%	
Stephen Peake	*Gre*	309	12.0%	

May 2006				*No change*
3. R.A.Max Boyce (R)	*LDm*	1000	42.5%	*LDm maj 512 (21.8%)*
Steven Mastin	*Con*	488	20.8%	
Simon Watkins	*Lab*	442	18.8%	
Sarah Peake	*Gre*	421	17.9%	

May 2007				*No change*
1. Diane Armstrong (R)	*LDm*	887	40.0%	*LDm maj 380 (17.1%)*
Steven Mastin	*Con*	507	22.9%	
Simon Watkins	*Lab*	451	20.4%	
Sarah Peake	*Gre*	371	16.7%	

May 2008				*No change*
2. M.Ian Nimmo-Smith (R)	*LDm*	969	43.2%	*LDm maj 456 (20.3%)*
Steven Mastin	*Con*	513	22.9%	
Michael Sargeant	*Lab*	461	20.5%	
Sarah Peake	*Gre*	302	13.5%	

May 2010 (2 vacancies)				*No change*
3. R.A.Max Boyce (R)	*LDm*	1881	43.3%	
1. Damien Tunnacliffe	*LDm*	1559	35.9%	*LDm maj 358 (8.2%)*
Sarah Peake	*Gre*	1201	27.6%	
Paul McHugh	*Lab*	853	19.6%	
Michael Sargeant	*Lab*	836	19.2%	
Anette Karimi	*Con*	752	17.3%	
Stephen Peake	*Gre*	674	15.5%	
Jahanshah Karimi	*Con*	652	15.0%	

West Chesterton   (contd.)

May 2011				*No change*
1. Damien Tunnacliffe (R) *LDm*		1225	38.5%	*LDm maj 359 (11.3%)*
Michael Sargeant	*Lab*	866	27.2%	
Robert Yeatman	*Con*	577	18.1%	
Stephen Lintott	*Gre*	513	16.1%	

May 2012				*No change*
2. Michael Pitt	*LDm*	840	36.7%	*LDm maj 89 (3.9%)*
Michael Sargeant	*Lab*	751	32.8%	
James Strachan	*Con*	372	16.3%	
Oliver Perkins	*Gre*	325	14.2%	

May 2014				*No change*
3. Ysanne Austin	*LDm*	1294	39.6%	*LDm maj 19 (0.6%)*
Michael Sargeant	*Lab*	1275	39.0%	
James Strachan	*Con*	353	10.8%	
Shayne Mitchell	*Gre*	347	10.6%	

May 2015				*No change*
1. Damien Tunnacliffe (R) *LDm*		1618	36.9%	*LDm maj 78 (1.8%)*
Michael Sargeant	*Lab*	1540	35.2%	
Har Kaur	*Gre*	537	12.3%	
Linda Yeatman	*Con*	528	12.1%	
Mary King	*UKIP*	156	3.6%	

May 2016				*Lab gain from LDm*
2. Michael Sargeant	*Lab*	1417	46.7%	*Lab maj 260 (8.6%)*
Nichola Harrison	*LDm*	1157	38.1%	
John Bachelor	*Gre*	198	6.5%	
Simon Lee	*Con*	182	6.0%	
Celia Conway	*UKIP*	81	2.7%	

May 2018				*No change*
3. Jamie Dalzell	*LDm*	1349	44.2%	*LDm maj 121 (4.0%)*
Clare King	*Lab*	1228	40.2%	
Mike Harford	*Con*	275	9.0%	
Shayne Mitchell	*Gre*	203	6.6%	

West Chesterton   (contd.)

May 2019 *No change*
1. Damien Tunnacliffe (R) *LDm*   1444   50.5%   *LDm maj 511 (17.9%)*
Alex Skinner   *Lab*   933   32.7%
Shayne Mitchell   *Gre*   310   10.9%
Michael Harford   *Con*   170   6.0%

No elections in 2020 due to Covid-19 pandemic

General re-warding (see map, near end of book)

May 2021 (All up elections – 3 vacancies) *2 Lab 1 LDm*
1. Mike Sargeant (R)   *Lab*   1668   47.0%
2. Jocelynne Scutt   *Lab*   1514   42.6%
3. Jamie Dalzell (R)   *LDm*   1305   36.8%   *LDm maj 69 (1.9%)*
Richard Swift   *Lab*   1236   34.8%
Shahida Rahman   *LDm*   1057   29.8%
David Grace   *LDm*   1040   29.3%
Roger Giddings   *Gre*   634   17.9%
Har Hari Kaur   *Gre*   566   15.9%
Shayne Mitchell   *Gre*   469   13.2%
Michael Harford   *Con*   333   9.4%
Sam Hunt   *Con*   233   6.6%

May 2022 (2 vacancies) *Lab hold 1, gain 1*
3. Richard Swift   *Lab*   1390   43.7%
1. Sam Carling   *Lab*   1229   38.7%   *Lab maj 58 (1.8%)*
Jamie Dalzell (R)   *LDm*   1171   36.8%
Shahida Rahman   *LDm*   970   30.5%
Shayne Mitchell   *Gre*   389   12.2%
Emma Garnett   *Gre*   337   10.6%
Jason Scott-Warren   *Ind*   294   9.3%
Jean-Ann Bartlett   *Con*   232   7.3%
Michael Harford   *Con*   191   6.0%

May 2023 *No change*
2.Rachel Wade   *Lab*   1314   42.4%   *Lab maj 306 (9.9%)*
Jamie Dalzell   *LDm*   1008   32.6%
Michael Harford   *Con*   412   13.3%
Shayne Mitchell   *Gre*   362   11.7%

West Chesterton   (contd.)

May 2024   *No change*
1.Sam Carling (R)	*Lab*	1290	42.9%	*Lab maj 208 (6.9%)*
Jamie Dalzell	*LDm*	1082	36.0%	
Shayne Mitchell	*Gre*	397	13.2%	
Michael Harford	*Con*	236	7.9%	

May 2025 (byelection)   *Ldm gain*
1.Jamie Dalzell	*LDm*	1204	38.5%	*LDm maj 174 (5.6%)*
Rosy Greenlees	*Lab*	1030	33.0%	
Hannah Copley	*Gre*	533	17.1%	
Tommy Brace	*Rfm*	197	6.3%	
Michael Harford	Con	160	5.1%	

May 2026   *No change*
Richard Swift (R)	*Lab*	1080	31.0%	*Lab maj 74 (2.1%)*
Guy Mills	*LDm*	1006	28.9%	
Hannah Copley	*Gre*	930	26.7%	
Geoff Leach	*Rfm*	202	5.8%	
Mike Harford	*Con*	147	4.2%	
Nick Picton	*Ind*	121	3.5%	

Ward maps

As populations of different wards varied, the ward boundaries were, from time to time, altered. This changed the electorate for each ward, and was apt to have an effect on voting patterns.

- Map of wards from 1912 to 1935
  (before the election results in this book)

- Map of wards from 1935 to 1968

- Map of wards from 1968 to 1976

- Map of wards from 1976 to 2004

- Map of wards from 2004 to 2021

- Map of wards from 2021

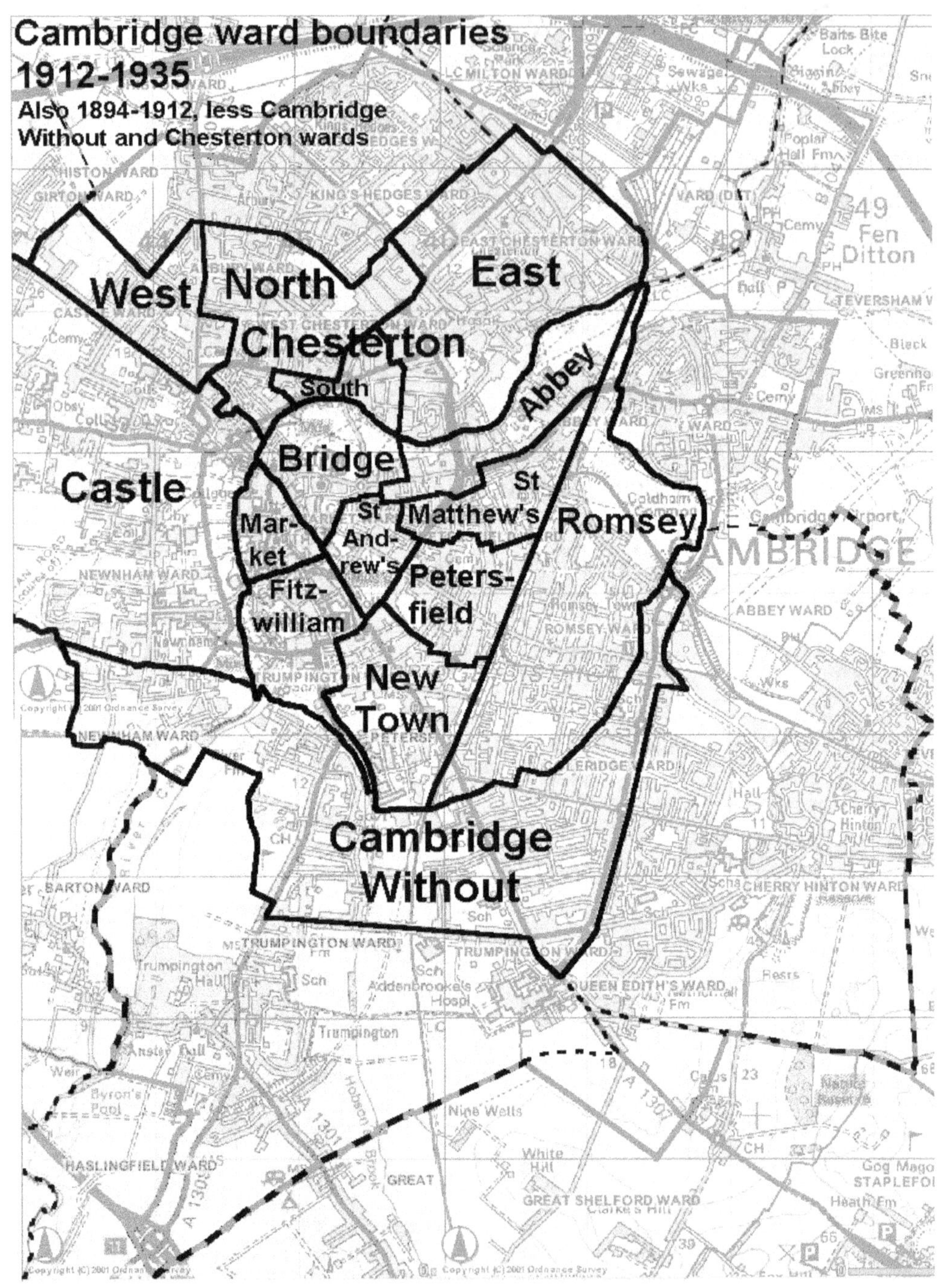

Map of wards from 1912 to 1935

This is before the election results in this book.

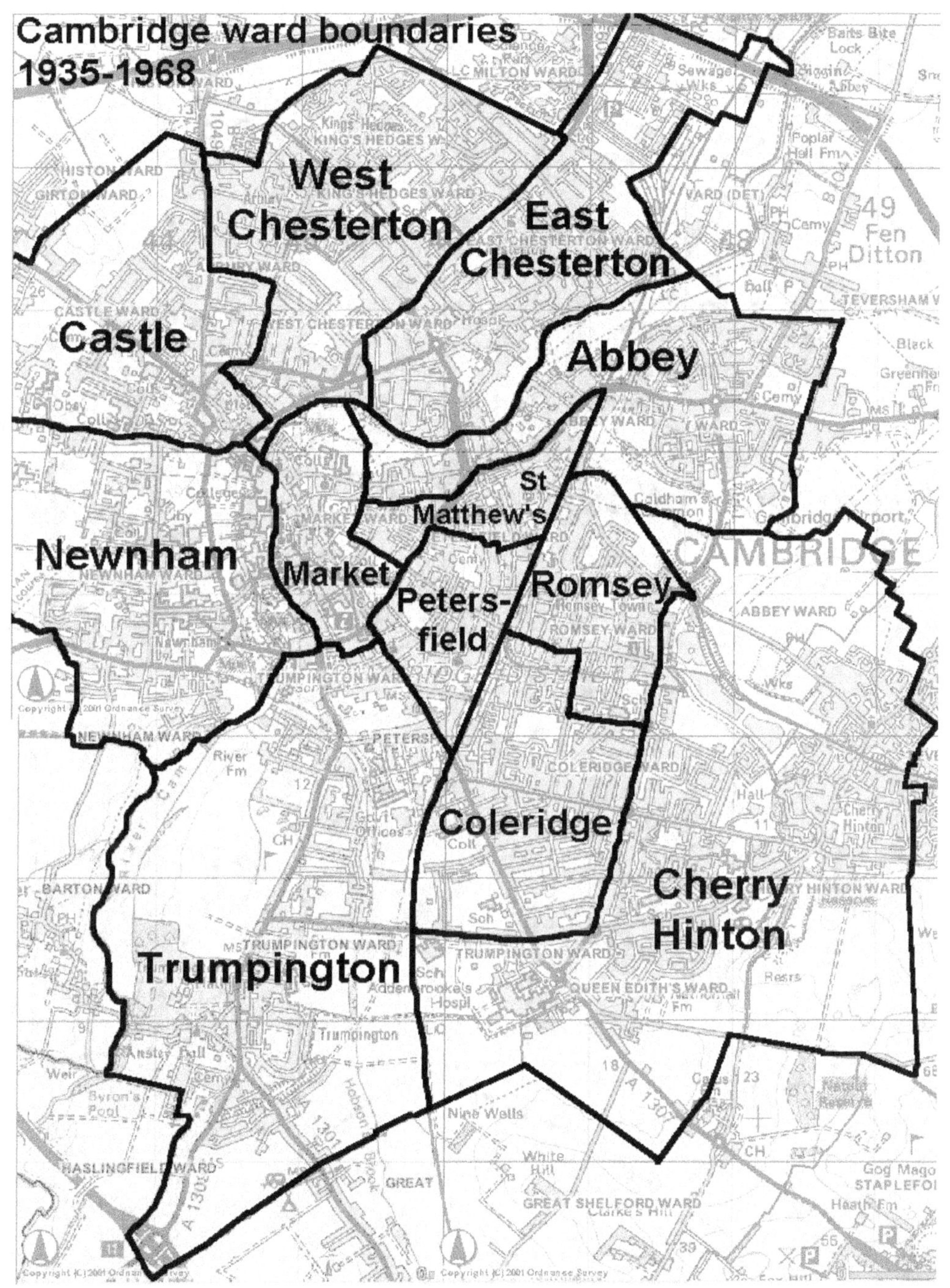

Map of wards from 1935 to 1968

There were all up elections in 1935.

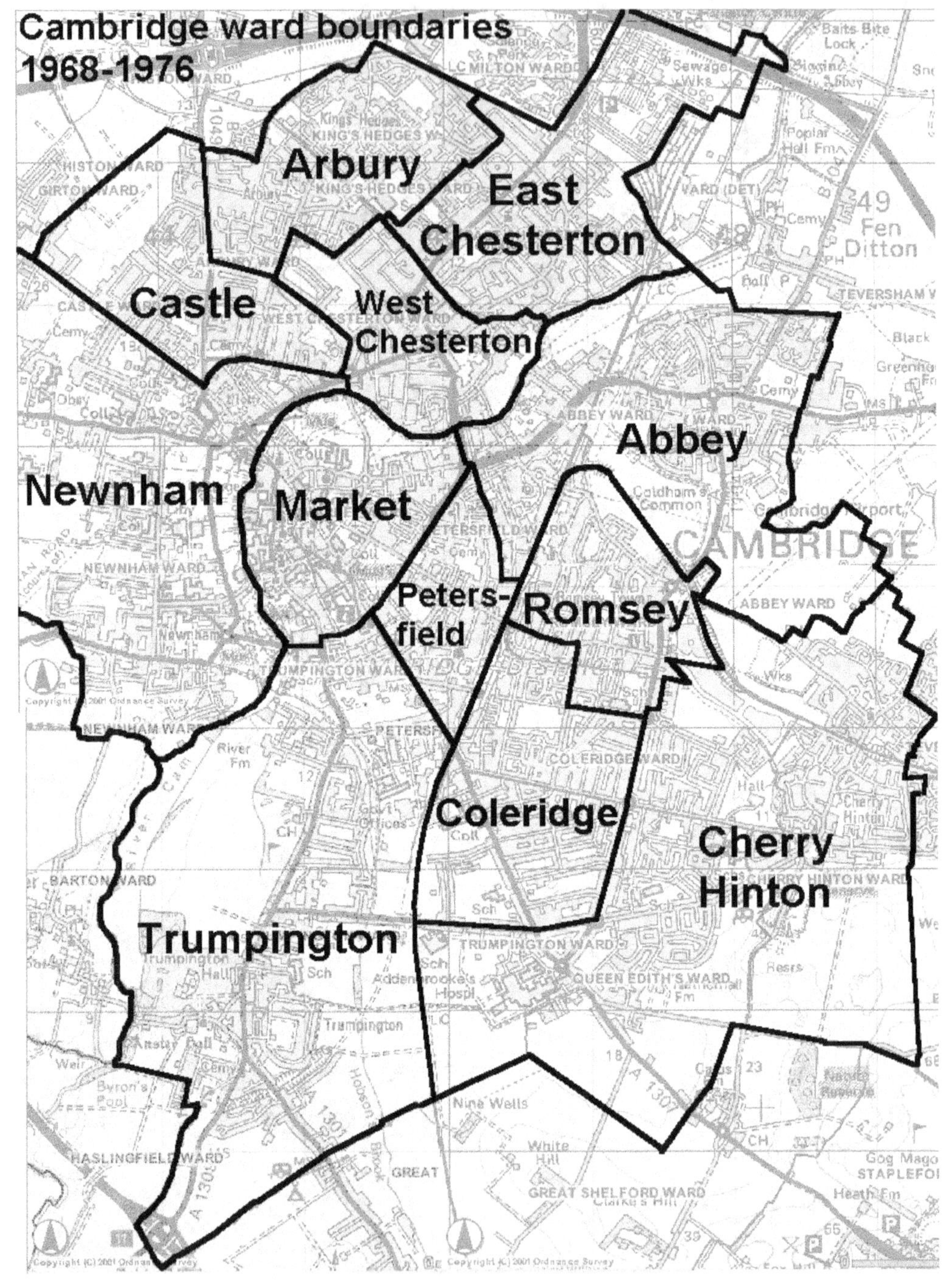

Map of wards from 1968 to 1976

There were no all up elections in 1968. There were all up elections in 1973.

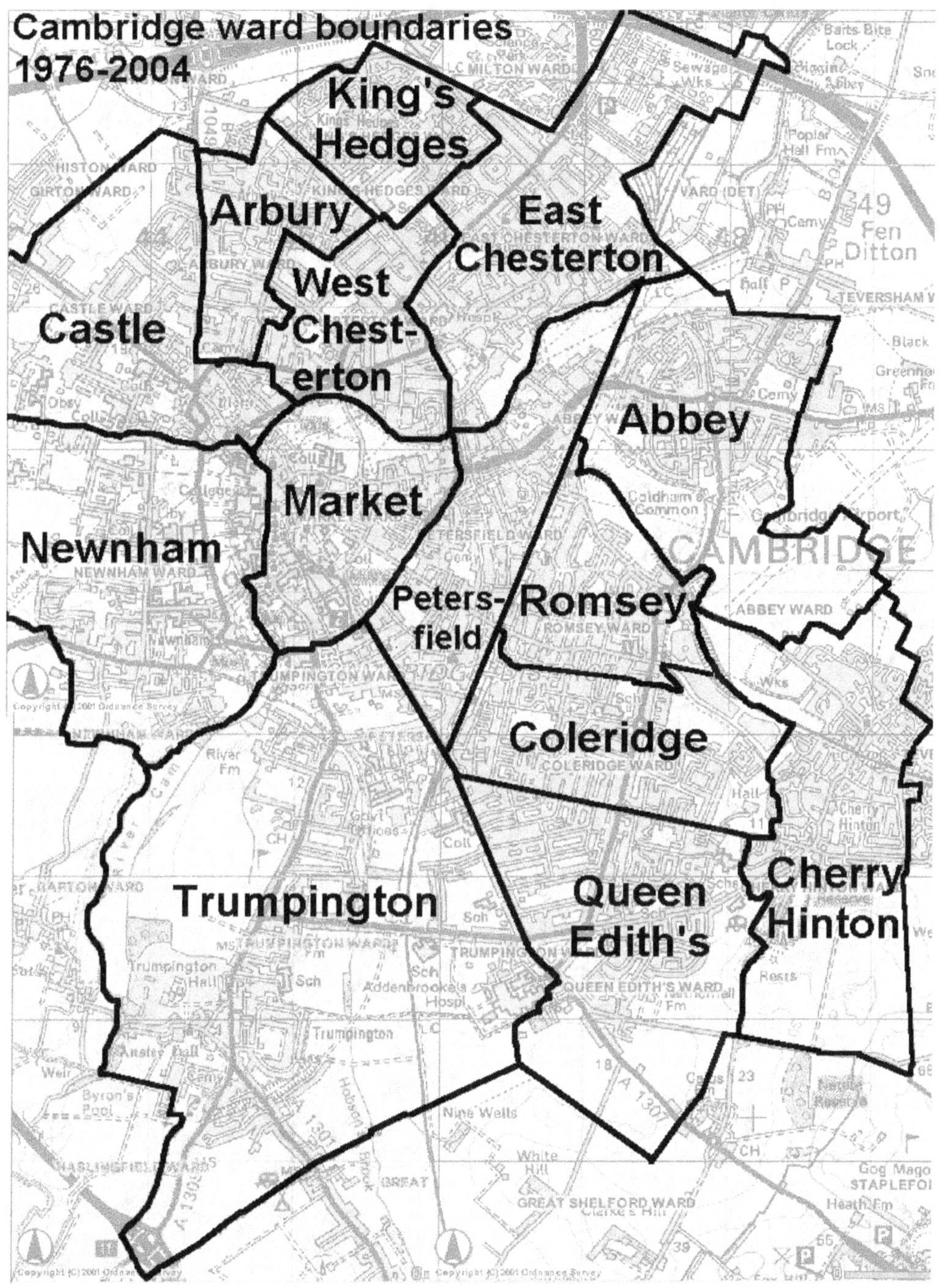

Map of wards from 1976 to 2004

There were all up elections in 1976.

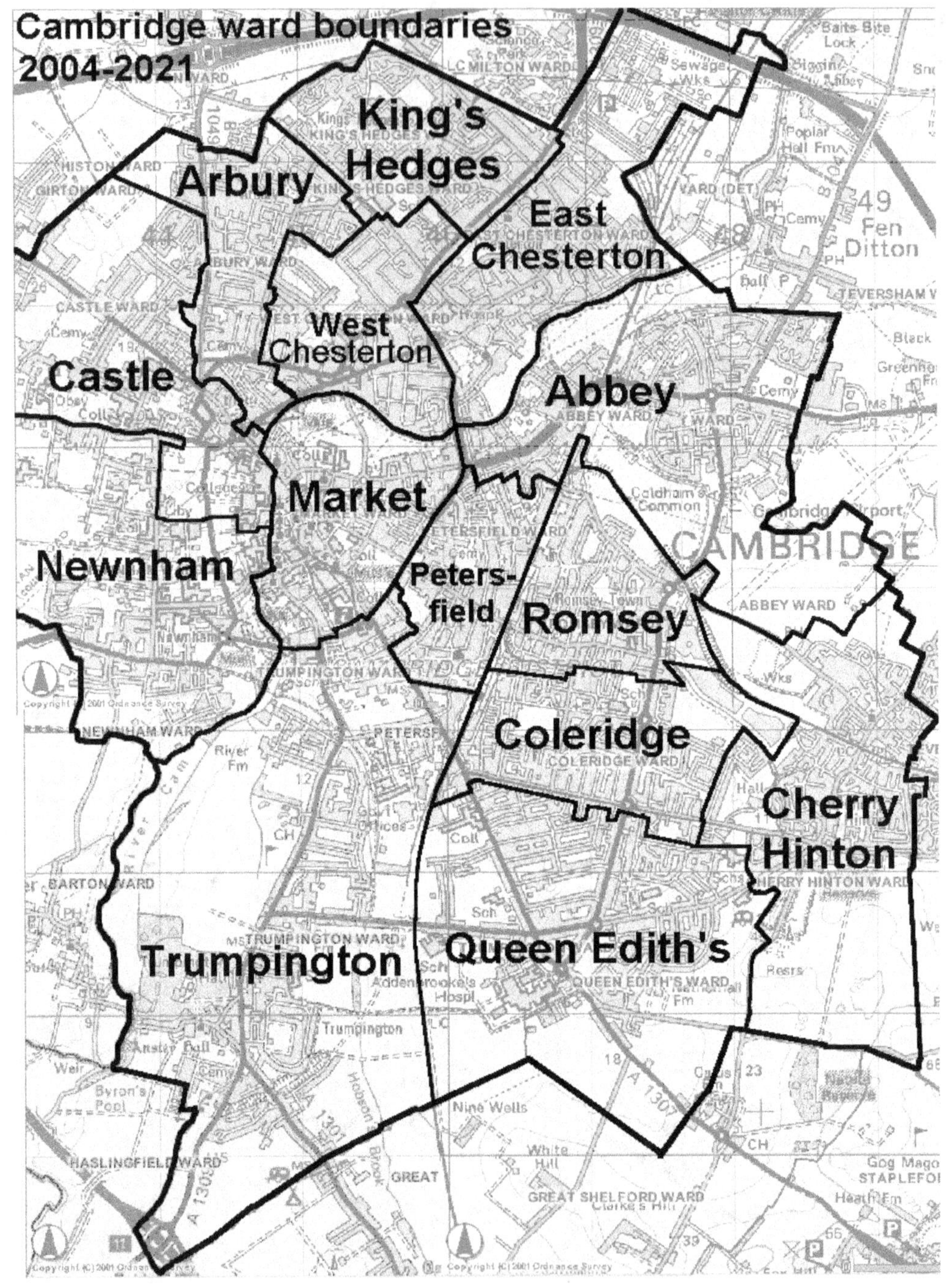

Map of wards from 2004-21

There were all up elections in 2004

Map of wards from 2021

There were all up elections in 2021 (postponed from 2020 due to Covid-19 pandemic)

Cambridge City Aldermen 1945-1972

Aldermen were appointed by the council. University aldermen were appointed by Cambridge University. These aldermen were part of the council and voted on matters the same as elected councillors. Aldermen were abolished by Local Government Act 1972.

Aldermen

1945-1950	Percy Squires	*Con*
1950-1963	George Nobbs	*Con*
1963-1972	P.Jack Warren	*Lab*
1945-1956	William Briggs	*Lab*
1956-1972	Thomas Amey	*Lab*
1945-1947	Herbert Wing	*Con*
1947-1964	Francis Priest	*Con*
1964-1970	Horace Ives	*Lib*
1970-1972	John Cuningham	*Con*
1945-1963	Alexander Spalding	*Con*
1963-1964	Leslie Jackson	*Con*
1964-1965	Denis Ash	*Lab*
1965-1970	Ernest Gill	*Lab*
1970-1972	Bernard Sargent	*Con*
1945-1950	Alex Wood	*Lab*
1950-1957	Clara Rackham	*Lab*
1957-1964	Howard Mallett	*Con*
1964-1967	Robert Davies	*Lab*
1967-1972	Stanley Bowles	*Con*
1945-1958	George Wilding	*Con*
1958-1969	Kelsey Kerridge	*Con*
1969-1972	Mabel Morse	*Con*
1945-1958	William Raynes	*Con*
1958-1972	C.Elliot Ridgeon	*Con*
1945-1949	Edward Brown	*Con*
1949-1958	Henry Langdon	*Con*
1958-1960	A.Leslie Symonds	*Lab*
1960-1967	Leonard Wordingham	*Lab*
1967-1970	Marcus Bradford	*Con*
1970-1972	Gladys Burn	*Con*
1945-1947	Ernest Peck	*Con*
1947-1967	Francis Doggett	*Con*
1967-1972	Herbert Finbow	*Con*
1945-1949	Jesse Harwood	*Con*
1949-1952	Herbert Banham	*Con*

<h1 style="text-align:center">Cambridge City Aldermen (contd.)</h1>

1952-1967	Stewart Bull	Con
1967-1972	George Dean	Con
1945-1949	Reuben Elsden	*Con*
1949-1967	Archibald Taylor	*Con*
1967-1969	M.Enid Henn	*Con*
1969-1972	William Crossman	*Con*
1945-1949	Albert Stubbs MP	*Lab*
1949-1963	William James	*Con*
1963-1972	Cecil Mole	*Con*

University Aldermen

1945-1964	Edward Halnan
1964-1967	J. Grantham
1967-1972	Peter Maitland
1945-1952	Sir Montagu Butler
1952-1972	Geoffrey Hickson

Mayors of Cambridge 1935-2021

The Mayor of Cambridge is chosen by Cambridge City Council. There are ceremonial duties, but the Mayor is still a councillor and may vote as such. The Mayor also has a casting vote when chairing a meeting.

The names repeat what appears (or will in due course appear) at the top of the stairs outside the Guildhall Council chamber. This includes the now somewhat quaint way of distinguishing the genders before 1998 - names for (untitled) women, initials for men.

The Mayor of Cambridge should not be confused with the Mayor of Cambridgeshire and Peterborough, who is directly elected, and is the leader of the Cambridgeshire and Peterborough Combined Authority.

Mayors of the Borough from 1935 to City status

1935-1936	H T Wing	*Con*
1936-1937	W L Briggs	*Lab*
1937-1938	E S Peck	*Con*
1938-1939	A A Spalding	*Con*
1939-1940	W J Wing	*Ind*
1940-1941	E O Brown	*Con*
1941-1942	Sir M Butler	*University*
1942-1943	Sir M Butler	*University*
1943-1944	W L Briggs	*Lab*
1944-1945	G Wilding	*Con*
1945-1946	Lady Bragg	*Ind*
1946-1947	F Doggett	*Con*
1947-1949	G F Hickson	*University*
1949-1950	W G James	*Con*

Mayors of the City to local government re-organisation in 1974

1950-1951	A C Taylor	*Con*
1951-1952	H O Langdon	*Con*
1952-1953	S T Bull	*Con*
1953-1954	T H Amey	*Lab*
1954-1955	H R Mallett	*Con*
1955-1956	E T Halnan	*University*
1956-1957	C E Ridgeon	*Con*
1957-1958	B J S White	*Con*
1958-1959	L D V Wordingham	*Lab*

Mayors of Cambridge (contd.)

1959-1960	W Cole	*Con*
1960-1961	C A Mole	*Con*
1961-1962	A Halcrow	*Con*
1962-1963	G F Hickson	*University*
1963-1964	J B Collins	*Con*
1964-1965	P J Warren	*Lab*
1965-1966	H G Ives	*Lib*
1966-1967	M N Bradford	*Con*
1967-1968	E A Gill	*Lab*
1968-1969	H C Finbow	*Con*
1969-1970	G Dean	*Con*
1970-1971	B Cooper	*University*
1971-1972	Jean Barker	*Con*
1972-1973	P C Wright	*Lab*
1973-1974	S C Bowles	*Con*

Mayors of the City since local government re-organisation in 1974

1974-1975	P J Warren	*Lab*
1975-1976	R May	*Lab*
1976-1977	R E Wright	*Con*
1977-1978	M J Garner	*Con*
1978-1979	A Molt	*Lab*
1979-1980	D R H Mackay	*Con*
1980-1981	Doris Howe	*Lab*
1981-1982	P O Reed	*Con*
1982-1983	P J Cowell	*Lab*
1983-1984	Betty Suckling	*Con*
1984-1985	E G Cowell	*Lab*
1985-1986	A J Johnson	*Con*
1986-1987	J R Woodhouse	*Lab*
1987-1988	T G W Sweeney	*Lab*
	P J Cowell	*Lab*
1988-1989	Lavena Hawes	*LDm*
1989-1990	J R Woodhouse	*Lab*
1990-1991	Dr G A Reid	*Con*
1991-1992	P J Cowell	*Lab*
1992-1993	B S Gardiner	*Lab*
1993-1994	A MacEachern	*Lab*
1994-1995	Joye Rosenstiel	*LDm*
1995-1996	Dr Sonja Froggett	*Con*

Mayors of Cambridge (contd.)

1996-1997	J Durrant	*Lab*
1997-1998	Daphne Roper	*Lab*
1998-1999	Peter Cowell	*Lab*
1999-2000	Richard Smith	*Lab*
2000-2001	Evelyn Knowles	*LDm*
2001-2002	Christopher Lakin	*LDm*
2002-2003	Philippa Slatter	*LDm*
2003-2004	David White	*LDm*
2004-2005	Robert Dryden	*Lab*
2005-2006	John Hipkin	*LDm*
2006-2007	Robert Dryden	*Lab*
2007-2008	Jenny Bailey	*LDm*
2008-2009	Michael Dixon	*LDm*
2009-2010	Russell McPherson	*Lab*
2010-2011	Sheila Stuart	*LDm*
2011-2012	Ian Nimmo Smith	*LDm*
2012-2013	Sheila Stuart	*LDm*
2013-2014	Paul Saunders	*LDm*
2014-2015	Gerri Bird	*Lab*
2015-2016	Robert Dryden	*Lab*
2016-2017	Jeremy Benstead	*Lab*
2017-2018	George Pippas	*LDm*
2018-2019	Nigel Gawthrope	*Lab*
	Gerri Bird	*Lab*
2019-2020	Gerri Bird	*Lab*
2020-2021	Russell McPherson	*Lab*
2021-2022	Russell McPherson	*Lab*
2022-2023	Mark Ashton	*Lab*
2023-2024	Jenny Gawthrope Wood	*Lab*
2024-2025	Baiju Thittala Varkey	*Lab*
2025-2026	Dinah Pounds	*Lab*
2026-2027	Maria Cleminson	*Gre*

Cambridge City Council Leaders since re-organisation in 1973

The Leader of the City Council is the leader of the majority party. This shows which party controls the council. The parties choose their own leaders.

Accession	Name	Party	Demise
June 1973	Peter Wright	*Lab*	Party lost control
May 1976	John Powley	*Con*	Lost seat
May 1979	Chris Gough-Goodman	*Con*	Party lost control
May 1980	Peter Wright	*Lab*	Voted out by group
May 1982	Chris Howard	*Lab*	Lost seat
May 1987	Mark Todd	*Lab*	Retired
May 1990	Simon Sedgwick-Jell	*Lab*	Retired
October 1994	Kevin Southernwood	*Lab*	Retired
February 1999	Ruth Bagnall	*Lab*	Party lost control
May 2000	David Howarth	*LDm*	Retired
July 2003	Ian Nimmo-Smith	*LDm*	Retired
May 2010	Sian Reid	*LDm*	Retired
May 2012	Tim Bick	*LDm*	Party lost control
June 2014	Lewis Herbert	*Lab*	Retired
December 2021	Anna Smith	*Lab*	Voted out by group
May 2023	Mike Davey	*Lab*	Retired
May 2025	Cameron Holloway	*Lab*	Lost seat
June 2026	Katie Thornburrow	*Lab*	

City of Cambridge Election turnouts

This graph shows the percentage turnout of voters in each election.
General election years increase turnout.

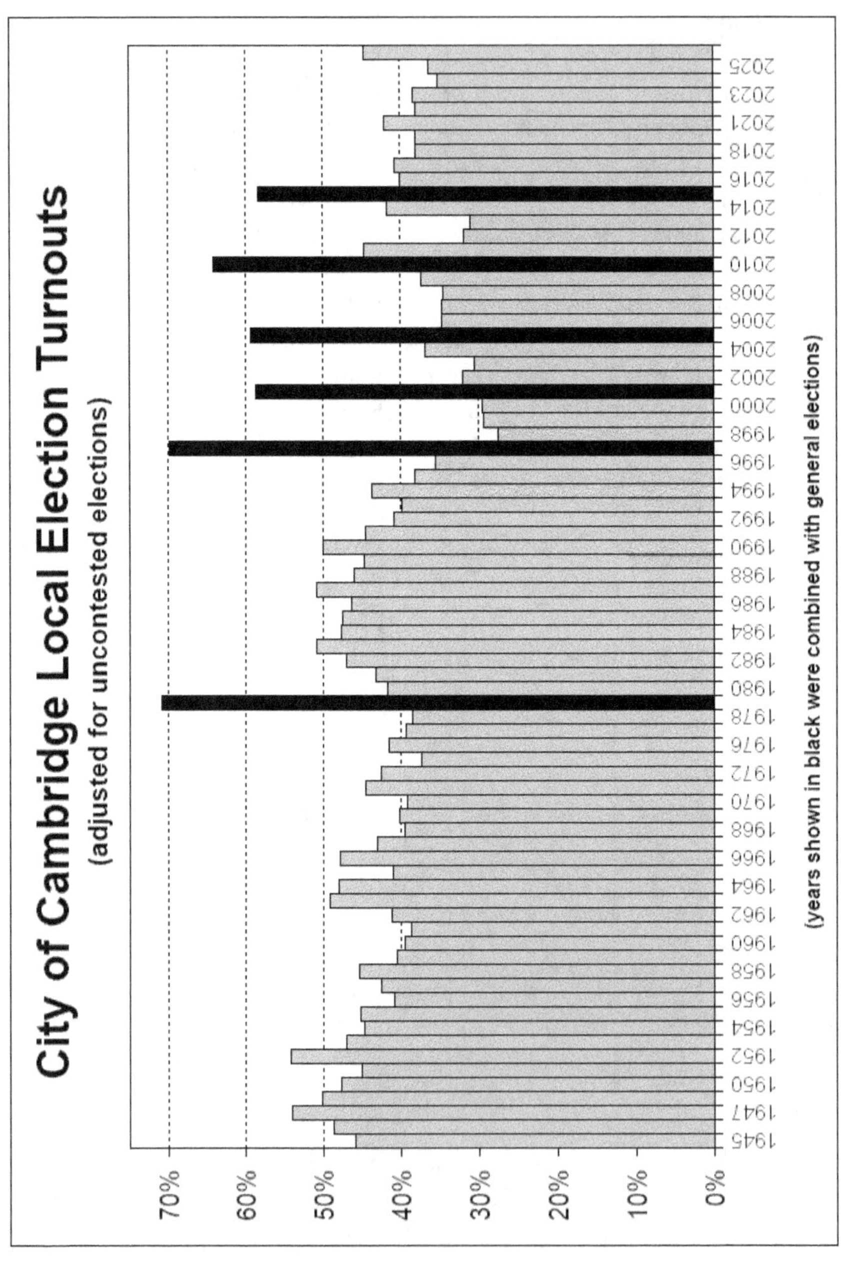

Composition of Cambridge City Council since 1945

These graphs show the numbers of councillors by party in the city council each year.
The line at 28 shows whether a party had an overall majority.

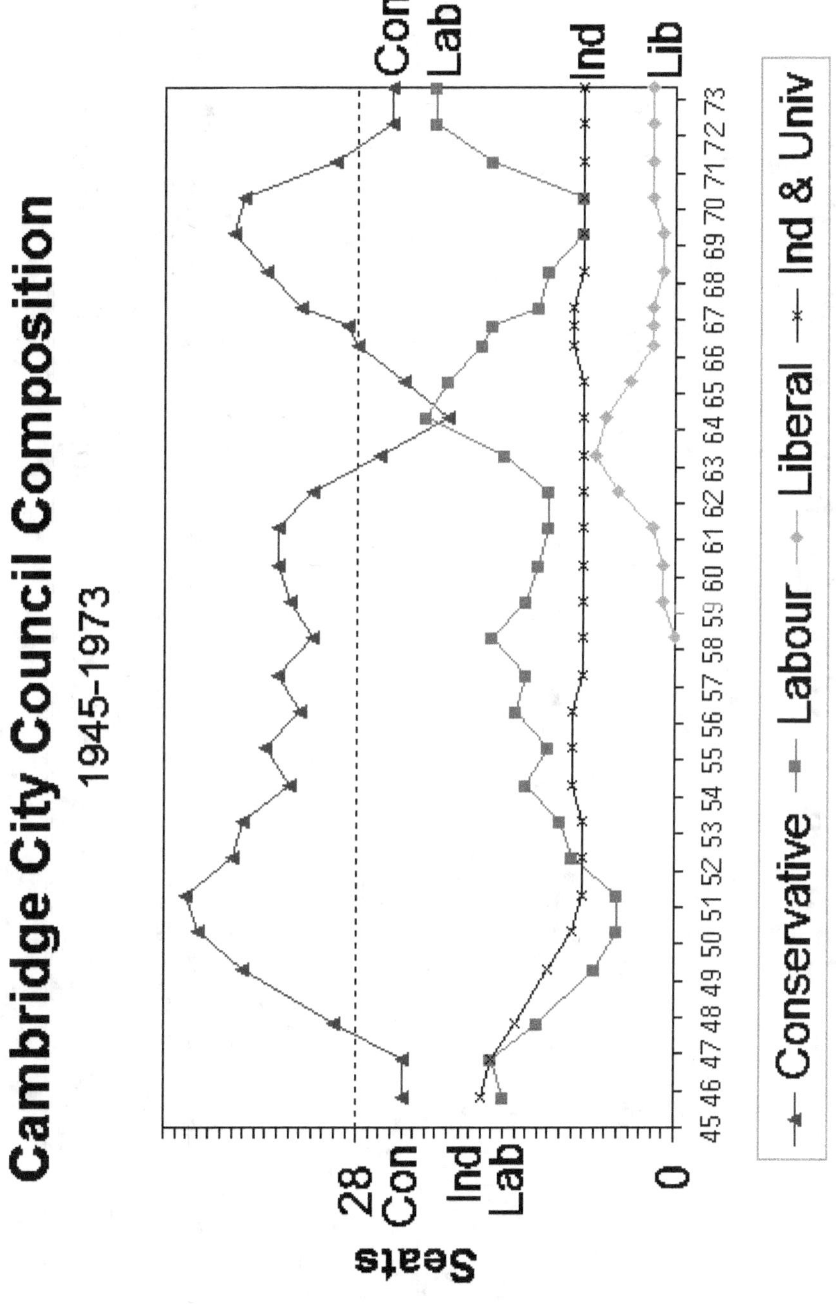

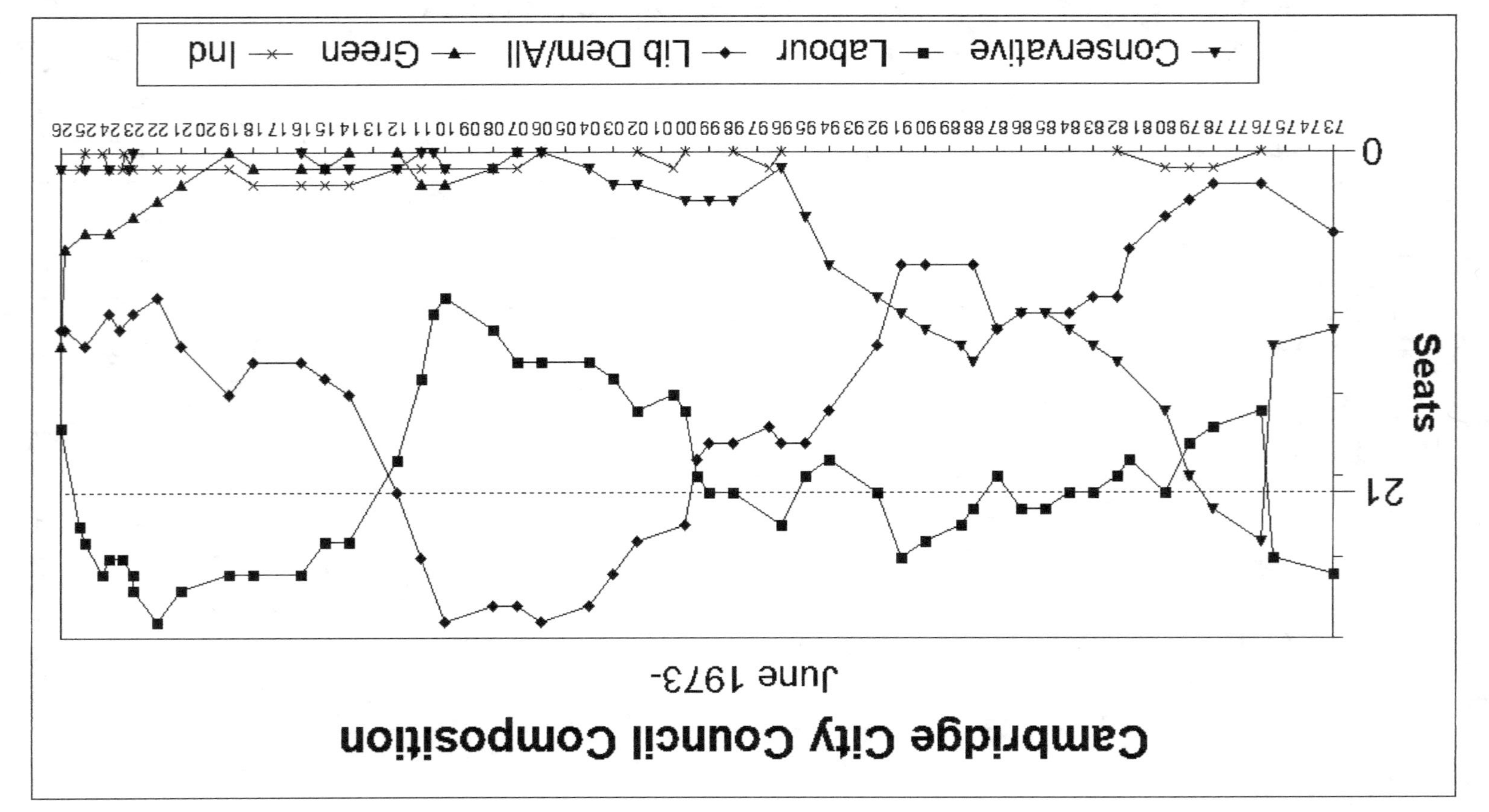

Cambridge City Council Composition
June 1973-
Seats
21
0
Conservative
Labour
Lib Dem/All
Green
Ind
73 74 75 76 77 78 79 80 81 82 83 84 85 86 87 88 89 90 91 92 93 94 95 96 97 98 99 00 01 02 03 04 05 06 07 08 09 10 11 12 13 14 15 16 17 18 19 20 21 22 23 24 25 26

Index of City councillors

This index lists all elected city councillors with their wards and dates they were elected, plus the aldermen. Please refer to the Ward Results to see further details, such as their party, their majority, and how long they served.

Margery	Abbott	East Chesterton 2012, 2016
Sonia	Abrams	St Matthew's 1962, 1965
Donald	Adey	East Chesterton 2003, 2004 - Trumpington 2016
Edrich	Adigun-Harris	Trumpington 2003, 2004
Salah	Al Bander	Trumpington 2008
Stanley	Allin	Cherry Hinton 1968
Harry	Ambrose	Coleridge 1935
Stanley	Ambrose	Cherry Hinton 1954
Thomas	Amey	Romsey 1945 1949, 1952, 1955 - Alderman 1956-1972
Douglas	Anderson	Coleridge 1976
Edgar	Anderson	East Chesterton 1955, 1958
Edward	Andrews	Trumpington 1945
Valerie	Antopolski	East Chesterton 1990
Diane	Armstrong	West Chesterton 2004, 2007
Henry	Arnold	Abbey 1935, 1938
Arthur	Arundale	Petersfield 1956, 1958, 1961
Dennis	Ash	Abbey 1957, 1960, 1963 - Alderman 1964-1965
Mark	Ashton	Cherry Hinton 2011, 2015, 2019, 2021, 2024
Neville	Auker	Castle 1966, 1968, 1971, 1973
Ysanne	Austin	West Chesterton 2014
Nicholas	Avery	Trumpington 2014
E.Ruth	Bagnall	Coleridge 1994, 1998, 2002
Dave	Baigent	Romsey 2014, 2018, 2021, 2024
Sarah	Baigent	Castle 2021
Cyril	Bailey	Coleridge 1951, 1954
Frank	Bailey	St Matthew's 1954, 1957
Jennifer	Bailey	East Chesterton 2002, 2004
Joyce	Baird	Newnham 1992
Alan	Baker	Queen Edith's 2002, 2003, 2004, 2006
Geoffrey	Baker	St Matthew's 1952
Jessie	Ball	Coleridge 1990
Cora	Banham	East Chesterton 1949, 1951
Herbert	Banham	East Chesterton 1939, 1947 - Alderman 1949-1952
Colin	Barker	Cherry Hinton 1978
Jean	Barker	Trumpington 1963, 1965, 1968, 1971
Anthony	Barnes	Abbey 1986, 1990, 1994

Index of City councillors (contd.)

John	Cuningham	Market 1966, 1968 - Alderman 1970-1972
James	Curley	Cherry Hinton 1958
Jean	Currie	Trumpington 2000
Ernest	Cutting	Abbey 1945, 1942

Jamie	Dalzell	West Chesterton 2018, 2021, 2025
Nora	David	Petersfield 1964 - Romsey 1968, 1971
Robert	Davies	East Chesterton 1954, 1957, 1960, 1963
"	"	- Alderman 1964-1967
Haf	Davies	Abbey 2019, 2021
Sam	Davies	Queen Edith's 2021
Harry	Davis	Petersfield 1950, 1952, 1955
Mike	Davey	Petersfield 2019, 2021, 2024
Euphemia Davison		Abbey 1963, 1965
Sefira	Davison	Arbury 2026
Peter	Day	East Chesterton 1986
Harold	De Ste Croix	West Chesterton 1950, 1952, 1955
George	Dean	Castle 1957, 1958, 1961, 1964, 1967 - Alderman 1967-1972
Donald	Denton-Smith	Cherry Hinton 1946, 1951
I.Paul	Diamond	Coleridge 1991
Arthur	Dilley	Trumpington 1935, 1938
Iva	Divkovic	Arbury 2022
Michael Dixon		Market 1999, 2003, 2004, 2007
Rev.Victor Dixon		St Matthew's 1966
Arthur	Doggett	Cherry Hinton 1935, 1937
Francis	Doggett	Castle 1935, 1937, 1946 - Alderman 1947-1967
Sylvia	Dolby	Queen Edith's 1976, 1979, 1983
Donald	Douglas	Trumpington 1998
Louise	Downham	King's Hedges 2003, 2004
Robert	Dryden	Cherry Hinton 1995, 1999, 2003, 2004, 2008, 2012, 2016,
"	"	2021, 2023
Andrew	Duff	Castle 1982, 1986
John	Durrant	Abbey 1987, 1991, 1995, 1999, 2003, 2004

Hazel	Eagle	Trumpington 1996
Peter	Eden	East Chesterton 1964
George	Edwards	East Chesterton 1937, 1946, 1950
Graham	Edwards	Market 1976
"	"	- Queen Edith's 1978, 1980, 1984, 1988, 1992, 1996
Robert	Edwards	Newnham 1973, 1976
Stanley	Edwards	Cherry Hinton1956, 1959

The data in this book comes from by Colin Rosenstiel's website

www.cambridgeelections.org.uk

Colin was a city councillor in Market for many years. He was fascinated by elections and the electoral process, and felt that there should be a record of the local Cambridge results. He died in 2018. This book is intended as a tribute to him.

This book covers the city council. The website covers more, including the city wards of the county council and more analysis of the data, so go to the website for that. It is kept up-to-date by Keith Edkins.

Although every effort has been made to ensure the accuracy of this data, mistakes are probably inevitable. I apologise for these, especially for errors produced by me when I reformatted the data to create this book.

Jo Edkins (editor)

The following comes from Colin Rosenstiel's own introduction to his website:

Electoral History

Cambridge City Council has had 42 councillors since 1935. Initially 12 wards each elected 3 councillors and there were 6 University councillors. All councillors served three-year terms, one third retiring each year, one in each ward plus two of the University councillors. In addition there were 14 aldermen, including 2 University aldermen. Aldermen were appointed by the councillors for six-year terms, half retiring every three years.

The ward boundaries were unchanged from 1935 until 1968 when the inner-city St Matthew's Ward was abolished, most of its electorate being divided between Market and Petersfield, and its councillors allocated to the new Arbury Ward, which was created, mostly from West Chesterton, to represent the growing suburban estates there. Minor changes were made to all the other wards except Coleridge. In 1971, most students became eligible to vote for the first time, with dramatic effects on the electorates of some wards, especially Market and Newnham.

Local Government Re-organisation

After the 1973 Local Government re-organisation, the City Council retained 42 councillors, all now elected. Initially they were elected from the same 12 wards, each being allocated between 2 and 5 councillors in proportion to its electorate, all for a three-year term.

The 1976 City election started a new system of retirement by thirds, following the creation of 14 new wards with changed boundaries. City elections are now held in 3 years out of 4, with councillors serving 4 year terms. (In the fourth year County elections are held.)

Another watershed was crossed in 2004 when the City Council had another election for the whole council on new boundaries, as in 1976. The same 14 wards continue but with changed boundaries. The members elected in 2004 retired by thirds in 2006, 2007 and 2008.

Ward boundaries were scheduled to change again in 2020, still retaining the same 14 names. In the event, this was delayed until 2021 because of the Covid-19 pandemic. The members elected in 2021 retired by thirds in 2022, 2023 and 2024.

Research and technical details

The information on these pages was collected from first-hand records taken at election counts since 1969 and from sources (mainly the Cambridge Evening News) in the Cambridgeshire collection of the Cambridge Central Library. I acknowledge with thanks the assistance and encouragement of Mike Petty and Chris Jakes of that library over many years.